GET OUT
OF THE
BOAT

Dr. J. Thomas Swanner, IV

GET OUT OF THE BOAT

Dr. J. Thomas Swanner, IV

GET OUT OF THE BOAT
ISBN: 978-1-941173-57-2
Copyright © 2024 by Dr. J. Thomas Swanner IV, D. Min.

All rights reserved. No part of this book may be reproduced, stored in a retrieval system or transmitted in any way by any means—electronic, mechanical, photocopy, recording or otherwise—without the prior permission of the copyright holder, except for brief quotations as provided by USA copyright law.

Published by
Olive Press
צחר זית
Publisher
www.olivepresspublisher.com

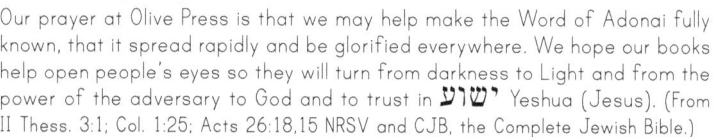

Our prayer at Olive Press is that we may help make the Word of Adonai fully known, that it spread rapidly and be glorified everywhere. We hope our books help open people's eyes so they will turn from darkness to Light and from the power of the adversary to God and to trust in ישוע Yeshua (Jesus). (From II Thess. 3:1; Col. 1:25; Acts 26:18,15 NRSV and CJB, the Complete Jewish Bible.)

Credits: Front and back cover artwork © 2024 by Annie West, Dallas, Texas.
Artwork on pages 47, 50, 55, 58 © 2024 by Karen Van Lieu, Nebraska.
Other images are from: TeachchildrenaboutChrist.com, p. 16; Getdrawings.com, p. 23; Vecteezy.com, pp. 28, 27, 111; VectorStock.com, p. 30; Freepik.com, pp. 36, 40, 223; Pixtastock.com, p. 42, 118, 182, 196, 203, 223; en.AC-illust.com, p. 64, 69, 126, 147; kindpng.com, p. 78; Pixy.org, p. 90; Judaicawebstore.com, p. 105; Etsy.com, p. 109; Clipartmag.com, p. 124; iStockphoto.com, p. 120. Used by permission. For others, the original source is unknown.

In honor to, all pronouns referring to the Trinity are capitalized; satan's names are not.

All Scripture unless otherwise marked are taken from the *Holy Bible, New International Version*. Copyright © 1973, 1978, 1984 by International Bible Society. All rights reserved.

Scripture quotations marked

AMPC are taken from the *Amplified Bible, Classic Edition*. Copyright © 1954, 1958, 1962, 1964, 1965, 1987 by The Lockman Foundation.

CSB are taken from *The Christian Standard Bible*. Copyright © 2017 by Holman Bible Publishers. Used by permission. Christian Standard Bible®, and CSB® are federally registered trademarks of Holman Bible Publishers, all rights reserved.

KJV are taken from the *Holy Bible King James Version*, public domain.

NKJV are taken from the *Holy Bible New King James Version*. Copyright © 1982 by Thomas Nelson, Inc. All rights reserved.

Dedicated to
my quiet supporter
and faithful friend,
Shortie

TABLE OF CONTENTS

Introduction   10

Section One   The Voice of the Lord   17
   Introduction   18
1. Scripture: Go through the Word of God
        to get to know the God of the Word   23
    A. Hear   28
    B. Read   29
    C. Study   30
        Observation   30
        Interpretation   33
        Application   35
    D. Memorize   36
    E. Meditate   36
    F. Copy   37
    G. Translate   38
    H. Recite   40

2. Saints: Those whom we know are hearing and
      following the Voice of the Lord)   42
    How Do We Leverage Saints into Voice Meters?   44

3. Sin: The conviction, cost, and forgiveness of sin
        is God's clearest Voice   47
   Conviction   48
   Forgiveness   49
      With Christ in John 13 and 14   49
      The Horrific Cost Required for Sin on the Cross   50
   What Killed Him?   53
   God Completely Connects with Fellow Forgivers.   57

4. Suffering: As the ultimate therapist, God intervenes
   in our suffering with His Presence, Power, Purpose,
   and the Pacifier of His comforting Word)   58

5. Songs (Psalms)   64

6. Sleep   69

7. Seraphs or Servants (Angels)   72
8. Self (Theophany or Christophany)   74
9. Situations or Circumstances   76
10. Still, Small Voice   78
    Conclusion   81

Section Two More Blessed to Forgive   83
  Introduction   84
    Three Components to God's Forgiveness   87
    Five Steps to Biblical Forgiveness   88
11. The Goal of Biblical Forgiveness   90
    Eight Forgiveness Truths in the Model Prayer   91
    Three Points of the Pure Gospel   96
    The Debt of Sin   97
12. The Five Steps of the Kenosis   100
    The Same Five Steps Demonstrated   103
    The Climax of it All   109
13. Human Alternatives to Forgiveness   111
    Overlooking the Offense, (not really)   112
    Brooding   112
    Ignoring the Offense and/or the Offender   112
    Going to Your Happy Place   113
    Talking About the Offense with Others   114
    Excusing the Offense for Whatever Reason   114
    Belittling the Offender   115
    Disparaging Yourself because of the Offense, as if You Deserved the Offense   115
    When We Need to Sound Spiritual, We Say We Will Pray About It   116
    We Label the Offense "Abuse"   116
14. The Balance of Guilt and Bitterness   118

15. God's Standard, The Lord's Prayer — 124
16. Five Steps of Forgiveness — 126
    Step One: Focus on the Offense — 127
    Step Two: Give the Offense and the Offender to Christ — 129
    Step Three: Thank God for the Offense — 131
    Step Four: Forgive During the Offense — 134
    Step Five: Change Your Version of the Offense from Victim to Victor — 137
17. Forgiving Yourself — 140
18. Forgiveness and Suffering — 144
19. The Other Side of Forgiveness — 146
20. The Evangelistic Challenge — 148
21. Questions and Answers — 150

Section Three Two by Two Leadership — 153
    Introduction — 154
        Three categories of Problems Facing Christian Leaders Today. — 157
22. Biblical and Historical Foundations — 161
    Biblical History of Leadership Partnerships — 162
    Not Good for Man to be Alone — 163
    Redemption from Slavery to Sin — 165
    Moses and Aaron — 166
    Kings and Advisors — 167
    No Hierarchy — 169
    The Purpose is Multiplication — 170
    Paraklete — 171
    The Early Church — 174
    The Church Age — 174
        Replacement Outcome — 175
        Partner Outcome — 176
    Chapter Summary — 179

23. Comparing and Contrasting Shared
     Leadership in Various Fields   180
    Shared Leadership in Nursing   181
        Four Constructs   181
    Two-Getherness   187
    Shared Leadership in Christian Ministry   190

24. The Church Case Study   194

25. The Two-By-Two Leadership Model
     For Christian Leadership   201
    The Two-by-Two Model   202
    Paul and Barnabas   203
    Identifying Leaders   207
        Born or Made?   207
        In Small Groups   208
    Development and Training of Leaders   209
    Leadership Training Curriculum   211

26. Fourteen Steps for Transitioning a
     Ministry to the Two By Two
     Leadership Model   213
    The Fourteen Steps   214
    Summary   220

Bibliography   222

Introduction

A couple of years ago I discovered that Jesus' first and last words to Peter were the same two words (in English). These two simple words had a major impact on Peter's life. After hearing these words the first time, Peter drastically changed his life and occupation. Jesus did not speak these words to Peter only, but also to almost everyone during His active earthly ministry.

Like Peter, most of the other people who heard Jesus utter these two words were drastically changed. The reason they were changed was because these two words were a command. If the person who heard this command was wise and radical enough to obey, they were blessed with a life of adventure and purpose. If, however, the hearer was foolish enough to disregard this command…we are not given too many details about these people's broken lives.

Many of you may have guessed what this two-word command was. Sometimes this command was couched in longer sentences, but the two-word core of the command came through time after time, "Follow Me." In every case, the various individual responses were polarizing. If a person did follow Christ, they typically left everything and followed. When a person did not obey Christ, they often did so violently. When these disobedient people were further confronted with the cost of following Christ (eating His body; drinking His blood), they rejected Him en mass (John 6).

This command made perfect sense at the beginning of Christ's ministry. Jesus gave this command to Peter as He began to walk the dusty roads in Galilee. It would be easy to follow in the footsteps that Jesus left in the dust on those roads. However, the

Introduction

fact that Jesus commanded Peter to follow Him shortly before He went back to the Father requires deeper understanding.

Peter would not have been able to follow Jesus as He Ascended into the heavens, at least not until his own execution. Obviously, it was more complicated to follow Christ after His Ascension. The specific steps that Peter took in response to this last command were recorded in the early chapters of the book of Acts. Taking these steps guided Peter to set the proverbial DNA and the actual formation of the early church.

One of the more imaginative paths that Jesus walked during His earthly ministry was the one across the Sea of Galilee. This took place on a dark and stormy night. (I remember the cartoon character, Snoopy, writing this sentence.) The story was recorded in three of the four Gospels (Matthew 14, Mark 6, and John 6). The disciples were in a boat, rowing for their lives against the storm. When they saw Jesus walking by, they thought He was a ghost. He assured them that He was not a ghost, but rather their master. Peter asked permission to come out of the boat, onto the water. Jesus granted this request (another instance of "Follow Me" implied). Peter walked with Jesus on the water for a short time.

Jesus is still walking imaginative paths today. He expects us to follow Him even though we cannot see His dusty footprints. Following Jesus on these paths takes the kind of faith that Peter must have had when he climbed out of the boat. We need to imitate Peter in this as we learn to trust Christ day by day. Jesus has called us to an impossible task. He has called us to reach a very lost and dying world with His love, grace, and mercy.

This book is dedicated to that brave few who will take up Christ's call to follow Him, even though He cannot be seen. The series will cover such impossibilities as *forgiving for real, hearing the Lord's Voice,* and *deploying two by two.* This book is meant to launch readers into a daily connection with the Creator and Sustainer of the universe. It is not meant to supplant the Bible as God's primary communication tool. Rather, they are meant to contextualize God's eternal, authoritative Word. To be clear, I am saying that if you are not reading the Bible daily, put down this book and go read your Bible.

There are some duties that must be maintained while walking these impossible paths. These duties are often called disciplines and include things like *centering on Christ, praying in power*, going through the *Word of God* to get to know the *God of the Word, living in community* and *sharing the living Christ with others*. There are more disciplines. However, these four (prayer, the word, fellowship, and evangelism) along with keeping Christ at your center by obeying Him, have helped many to continue to follow behind Jesus.

Only one of the Gospel writers recorded the incident of Peter following Jesus onto the water. In the Gospel of Matthew, we read that when Jesus was walking by the boat on that dark and stormy night, Peter asked for permission to join Jesus as He walked on the water. Jesus consented to this, and Peter climbed out of the boat, beginning his stroll on that watery path. As the familiar story goes, he soon was swamped by the waves that had caught his attention. Many a preacher has made much of the fact that Peter began to sink. These heralds love to point out the various reasons for Peter's literal downfall on this occasion. None of them, however, has ever set one foot on a body of liquid water.

After much prayer and study, several clues have surfaced as to why Matthew was the only one to record this part of the larger event when Jesus walked on the water.

There is little doubt among Biblical scholars today that the Gospel of Mark was written by John-Mark after he spent much time learning at the feet of the apostle Peter. Yet, John-Mark did not include the detail of Peter joining Jesus on the water. This omission may be due to Peter's humility. He may have not told

Mark of his involvement in this miracle, or he may have instructed Mark to omit it.

The Apostle John, being Peter's beloved partner in ministry, may have also committed this omission in favor of Peter's humility. It may be that the two of them discussed it at some point, and then decided that it was not to be part of the narrative that they would provide. After all, John had another reason for writing his Gospel in the first place.

John wrote that he chose the seven miracles he recorded in his account of Jesus' life because these would best show that Jesus was the Messiah. He chose these seven miracles so that his readers could find life in believing in Jesus Christ (John 20:31). The detail of Peter walking on the water with Jesus was not included in John's account perhaps because this part of the story did not serve his purpose for writing his Gospel. It simply did not fit with the thesis of his account of the life of Christ. In the previous verse (20), John wrote that there were many things that he left out of his Gospel for the sake of brevity.

At this point, we must understand Peter's mind-set after the Lord rose from the dead. Peter had been forgiven much, so he loved Jesus very much. Meanwhile, he felt profoundly unworthy to be compared to Christ favorably. We can see this best when Peter was finally led to his own death on a cross. It is said that on that day, Peter asked to be crucified upside-down because he did not consider himself worthy to be crucified in the same way that Jesus was crucified.

It is not a far reach, then, to understand why John-Mark and the Apostle John did not include Peter's involvement in this miracle. Being actual authors and not robots, they had editorial control as to which stories they would include or exclude in their respective Gospels.

So those two Gospel writers who included the account of Jesus walking on the water had their reasons for omitting Peter's part in this miracle. Matthew, who was apparently under no such compulsion, did not hesitate to include Peter's role in his account of this story. Matthew 14:28 recorded Peter's challenge of the words that Jesus had just spoken. Jesus had just said that it was He, Himself, and that the disciples should not fear.

I am convinced that Matthew was quick to include this part of the story for one painful reason, his perspective. He was one of the other eleven followers of Jesus who remained in the boat. It is easy for some preachers to find fault with the mechanics or details of what Peter did. However, Matthew did not provide this account for us to take pot shots at Peter. He gave us this part of the story because he wanted us to be more like Peter and less like the others who stayed with him in the boat.

Matthew and the disciples stayed in the relative comfort of the endangered boat. They were clinging to the gun rails, hoping that the waves dashing against their faces would not swamp their boat. They witnessed Peter walking on top of those waves. They may have wondered if Jesus and Peter were planning to walk to the shore without them. If his lack of faith did not dawn on him then, it certainly did later as Matthew penned the story of his classmate (Peter) passing this test of faith.

During His earthly ministry, Jesus talked a lot about faith. Since faith is best seen in action, He also gave quizzes and tests. This was one of those tests. Peter is the only disciple who passed this test. I sometimes ask myself if I would pass such a test. I like to believe that I would pass. The situations that we find ourselves in today are very similar to the test that night. We cannot see Jesus' footprints. Many of His words to us are given as a still small Voice (*Voice Of the Lord* chapter 10). We are expected to know that it is the Lord speaking and to trust a Voice that we cannot hear with our physical ears.

Introduction

Once Peter realized that it was indeed the Lord speaking, he needed to have the courage to get out of the boat. This took quite a bit of nerve. Peter was a career fisherman. Fishing for a living is one of the most dangerous jobs. The biggest threat in this profession is leaving the boat. Peter must have had a courageous faith to go over the side the boat, especially during a storm.

There is little difference for us on this point. After we have discovered that the Lord has directed us to do something, we can do a risk assessment. The Lord always leads us into risk when teaching faith. It could be a real or imagined risk, but it is still risk. It is safe to say that following the Lord today is like walking on the water.

Please do not hear me say that any risky thing we do is the Lord testing our faith. Many misadventures have been undertaken with this belief. The balance of this book is dedicated to helping you see the difference between the Lord speaking and someone else speaking. Please understand that we must first be convinced that the Lord has spoken, *then* we must courageously act.

Section One

The Voice of the Lord

Section 1 The Voice of the Lord

Introduction

Jesus said that His sheep would know His Voice and follow Him (John 10). This is a very good definition of a disciple. **The goal in making a disciple is to cause people to hear the Lord's voice and do what He says.** Until this begins to happen, people are not fully following Christ. They may attend a service or commit to acts of service, and still not be disciples.

The first Psalm is a lovely reminder that the Word of the Lord is vital for blessed living. This Psalm reminds that it is very important to value the Voice of the Lord as shown in His Word, the Bible. Rather than consorting with wicked, sinning mockers, the blessed person delights in the law of the Lord. This person meditates on this Voice day and night. There is an interesting connection between the word for meditate and mumble. It is as though the blessed person goes around mumbling the Bible day and night. The overall point is that this person hears the Voice of the Lord as shown in the Bible.

Jeremiah 17:7-10 is a superb cross-reference to Psalm 1. Verse 8 paints the exact same word picture in the description of the tree. The interesting contrast to this passage with respect to Psalm 1 is the reason that this tree (and by extension the blessed person) experiences the blessings. There is a promised blessing here. The only question we should entertain is not concerning the veracity of the blessing (whether the Lord is true to His Word, or whether He is able to deliver it). Rather, the only question that we should ask is: Is this promised blessing based on our activity (conditional) or simply the Lord's grace (stand-alone)?

Both passages clearly show that this is a conditional promise rather than a stand-alone promise from the Lord. Both passages describe something that is done by the person that is blessed, which elicits the blessing from the Lord. The Psalm 1 passage says that the blessed person delights in the Bible. The Jeremiah passage says that the blessed person trusts in the Lord as opposed to trusting in the flesh (people). Right in the middle of this passage is the very famous verse 9, *"The heart is deceitful above all things and beyond cure. Who can understand it?"*

The next verse (10) shows that it is the Lord that knows our hearts and that despite our "good" intentions, our deeds reveal the truth therein. So, it is ultimately what we do that shows the Lord, us, and anyone else who is paying attention, whether our hearts and motives are pure and worthy of blessing. The particular area that the prophet Jeremiah focused on in the rest of this chapter (verse 19 to the end) was concerning the Sabbath day. It was as if the Lord was saying to those people that if they would just quit violating the Sabbath day regulations, the Lord would have mercy on them. Sadly, they did not and very few of them lived much longer.

I am not arguing that we are saved by works. Instead, I am saying that the second half of being a disciple is required. We must learn to obey what the Voice of the Lord tells us to do. This distinction (and the rest of whatever I happen to say) means that I am writing to believers in the Lord Jesus Christ. I am writing to people who have already found faith in Him and are working to be His *followers*.

Speaking of Jesus, He also weighed in heavily on this subject. At the end of the seventh chapter in the Gospel of Matthew, Jesus told a story of two builders. This story is known as the tail of the wise versus the foolish builders. At the end of the story, Jesus defined exactly how He concluded that one was wise and the other foolish. They both heard the Voice of the Lord. The only difference was that the wise one obeyed what he heard and the foolish one did not.

Book 1 The Voice of the Lord

So, we have heard from both testaments including a story from the Master Himself on this subject. **A disciple hears the Lord's voice and does what He says.** If you end up reading much of what I write, you will find that this is the theme of my life's message. If you happen to agree, I encourage you to sit back, relax, and keep reading. You might get a blessing or two. If you happen to disagree, you might just keep reading anyway. You might just get a blessing, as well.

The Bible is filled with stories of how the Lord introduced Himself to various individuals. It is interesting to note that after people met with God, they were never the same. The story of Jacob was a prime example.

Before his first encounter with God at Bethel, Jacob was known as a scheming deceiver. From the womb, Jacob was continually scrapping to get ahead. At the behest of his mother, he even went so far as to steal his older brother, Esau's, birthright, deceiving his blind elderly father in the process. He then ran (probably for his life) and stopped to catch his breath at a place called Bethel (the name means *House of God*) (Genesis 28). After a very vivid and dramatic dream, Jacob realized that the Lord was there (hence the name). God had promised Jacob that he would return to that place.

After this introduction to God (at Bethel), Jacob trusted the Lord, but only so far. It was as if he was trying to manipulate the Lord like he had tried to manipulate everyone else. His attempts to manipulate his family and in-laws had left him with few options. After He burned his proverbial bridges with his in-laws, he lost his welcome to live among them.

Jacob realized that he would need to meet with Esau, his brother. This meeting would be far from the typical Hollywood scene of two long lost brothers running into each other's embrace. Rather, it could have become a battlefield between their two houses. Jacob did all the kissing up to his brother that he could do in advance of their meeting, to avoid battle. However, the night before the big meeting, he was still fearful of what might happen the next morning. Would Esau kill the members of Jacob's family? Would he and his household be slaves by this time tomorrow?

The Lord knew Jacob's fears and arranged an even bigger meeting that night. It was the night when the Lord came to meet Jacob, in person. The Lord presented Himself as a man, ready to wrestle. Not fully knowing who this stranger was, Jacob fought with Him all night. When it was almost dawn, Jacob realized that it was the angel of the Lord (perhaps the pre-incarnate Christ).

Jacob put a hold on the man/angel that was very hard to break. Some wrestlers are very good at this. Jacob demanded a blessing from the Lord in exchange for releasing the hold. As the morning dawned, the Lord blessed Jacob. Jacob released the Lord from the hold. As He was leaving the Lord touched Jacob, and he was never the same again. God changed his name to Israel and injured his hip so that he limped for the rest of his life.

I have named this scenario and others like it, *self,* which happens to be number eight out of ten modes by which the Voice of the Lord has been heard. As in, "the Lord Himself shows up and speaks to some people." This Voice, however, was very rare and is no longer in use. Jesus Himself warned us not to believe that this Voice is from the Lord, in this age. We will discuss this in depth in chapter 8. The obvious implication of not relying on this Voice is that we need to be able to hear the other nine Voices even more clearly.

I recently re-visited the book of Deuteronomy in my personal study. I was shocked when I stumbled across chapter 4 with respect to the Voice of the Lord.

In an effort to stem the children of Israel's bent toward idolatry, Moses reminded the Nation of Israel that when they met the Lord at Sinai, they did not **see** God. They saw what He could **do** (Fire, Smoke, Billowing Clouds) but not Him. What they did

Section 1 The Voice of the Lord

experience, however, was the Lord's Voice. For this reason, it was imperative that they did not worship any form (idol) as a representative of God. To them He was simply a Voice that they needed to obey. Moses reminded them that because he **disobeyed** the Voice, he would not be entering the Promised Land.

So that we will be able to remember them, I have named and numbered the Voices. They are:

1. Scripture
2. Saints
3. Sin
4. Suffering
5. Songs
6. Sleep
7. Seraphs
8. Self
9. Circumstances
10. Still-Small Voice

It is my hope that we will move from number one, which is the most objective, to number ten, which is the most subjective. When we can hear the Lord's still small Voice, we can receive instructions for each day. This Voice, however, is the hardest to hear and the most often misunderstood. But when we use all the other Voices as tools, we can move with confidence in this one, as well.

1
Scripture

Go through the Word of God to get to know the God of the Word

There is a common misunderstanding with respect to Scripture. Most people think the Bible is a set of rules, given to us so we will stay in line. I was talking with a woman the other day that had a problem in this area. She said that she could not bring herself to obey a book that was written by men. Upon further investigation, I realized that it was not really the Bible that had her stymied, but men. She had been so abused by the male half of our species that anything associated with men was suspect or even despised.

Section 1 The Voice of the Lord

One of her misunderstandings about the Bible was that it was a rulebook given to take away our happiness. Specifically, she was certain that the Bible banned the use of methamphetamine for recreational consumption.

The Bible is not primarily a rulebook. It is a book that was designed to help us know the unknowable God. As for the meth abuse, I saved that discussion for another occasion shortly after her introduction to the Savior.

Theologians tell us that the Creator and Sustainer of the universe is wholly other. This means that God is beyond our ability to comprehend. Isaiah wrote, *"For my thoughts are not your thoughts, neither are your ways my ways,' declares the Lord. 'For as the heavens are higher than the earth, so are my ways higher than your ways and my thoughts than your thoughts'"* (Isaiah 55:8-9). God is so far beyond us, that if He did not reveal Himself to us, we would never have any hope of knowing Him.

In that same chapter, Isaiah wrote a beautiful description of the earth's water cycle and compared it to God's Word.

"As the rain and the snow come down from heaven, and do not return to it without watering the earth and making it bud and flourish, so that it yields seed for the sower and bread for the eater, so is my word that goes out from my mouth: It will not return to me empty, but will accomplish what I desire and achieve the purpose for which I sent it" (Isaiah 55:10-11).

When we put these two passages together (they come this way), it is easy to see that although the Lord is unknowable, He sent His Word to make Himself known. He sent His Word, then, to reverse the fact that He was unknowable to us. Why would He do this? Could it be true that He hates us and wants nothing to do with us? This seems unlikely. It is rather more likely that He wants to be close to us, so that we can be friends with Him.

There are three tools that God has used to reveal Himself. The **first** is by *general revelation, as seen in His creation.* The **second**

1 Scripture

is through *His written Word, the Bible*. The **third** is through the *Father's last Word, Jesus Christ*.

God made the universe and put clues in it to cause us to realize that He exists. The apostle Paul wrote of this in the first chapter of his letter to the Romans. In the twentieth verse we can read, *"For since the creation of the world God's invisible qualities—his eternal power and divine nature—have been clearly seen, being understood from what has been made, so that people are without excuse."*

God allowed His creation to reveal that He is very powerful. He also allowed nature to reveal a few other things about Him. One of these is that He is wise. Another is that He has the qualities of a person (mind, will, and emotion).

Even after He revealed these things to us through nature, God knew that we still would not know Him very well. At best, we would assume that He was bigger than us and because He was distant, that He does not like us. Many of us have assumed, further, that He wants to squash us like bugs. This assumes the worst about Him. I am learning that this is the philosophy of most people.

My friend, the meth user, reminded me of this the other day. She was sure that God was out to get her and was simply waiting for the right time to smash her. She got this idea from the religion under which she was raised. This is a problem with religion. It does not matter which religion, they all have the same message, "God is mad at you, and He will judge you someday."

The message of the Gospel of Jesus Christ is a very different message. The unknowable God wants us to know Him because He wants to show His love for us. This is why He made us in the first place. What kind of stupid god would make us, put up with our shortcomings, and die for us on a cruel cross just to smash us in the end? He did not make us for judgment, but to be the object of His deep affection. God loves you!

Section 1 The Voice of the Lord

Once we understand that God is on our side, it is easy to see that He did not make us to be His whipping boy. He made us to love us.

Anyone who is in love hopes that the person they love will reciprocate their love. This means we should love God in return. He has gone to great lengths to make sure we could love Him. Since this is the case, why do so many of us not love Him?

The second tool that God has employed to reveal Himself to us is His Word, the Bible.

It is hard to love someone that you do not know. The Bible was given to us so that we could know God. If all we knew about God were given to us through nature, it would be hard to intimately know Him well enough for love.

When I say that I love my mechanic, what I am saying is that I am glad that I can entrust my car to him for servicing. He does the job quickly and inexpensively. He also does not try to fix things that are not broken to fatten his wallet. I also "love" him because he provides a car for me to drive when he is working on my car.

However, when my wife says that she loves her plumber with all her heart, I feel warmth in my soul. By the way, I am the only plumber she has ever employed.

What did it take for my wife to love her plumber on an infinitely deeper level than I love my mechanic? Intimate knowledge. She not only knows *about me, she knows me*. The same is true of our knowledge of the Lord. The more we know Him, the more we love Him. It is interesting to note that the primary command from the Lord is for us to love Him with all our heart, mind, soul, and strength. Could it be that the first step in keeping this command is reading our Bible?

Many of us, sadly, have settled for the level of intimacy with the Lord that I have with my mechanic. This has left us listless and empty. We lack purpose; most of us are fairly bored. This hardly seems like the abundant, joy-filled life that Jesus described (John 10:10 CSB).

1 Scripture

We need to seek to know the Lord even deeper than my wife could ever know me.

Since the Bible is more like a love letter than a legislative treatise, we need to begin to treat it as such.

I grew up in the age of telephones. Letters were never something that I valued. If I wanted to talk to someone, it did not matter that they were several thousand miles away; I would spare no expense as I reversed the charges. (For those of you who do not know, that means that the person I was calling would pay for the call.) I would talk until I had nothing else to say and then I would let them talk for a few minutes so that they would feel good about the charges being reversed. I never have valued a written word from my loved ones.

My wife, Angel, however, is another story. She would rather get a hand-written letter from a loved one than to talk on the phone. I have never understood this until lately. Recently, I have come to realize that a letter is longer lasting than a call or a meal or flowers. My letter is something she can pull out in ten years to see how much I loved her back then. This reminds her that I am very much in love with her, now. There is power in the written word.

The love letter that the Lord has provided has shown us His heart, that He loves us deeply. It is something that we can pull out and reread, pouring over its contents until we come to understand and know the author. The Bible's author is none other than Almighty God. God used human instruments in writing His love letter, but He absolutely is the author.

The Word of God is by far the most objective Voice of the Lord. It is the Voice by which all other Voices are tested. The only way to know that it is the Lord speaking is to know *His first Voice*, **the Bible**. It may be rightly presumed that if you do not know the Bible, you do not know what God sounds like.

The Bible is God's inerrant Word. It is flawless. There are no verifiable contradictions in it. It is a unit and it agrees with itself.

Section 1 The Voice of the Lord

Internal consistency is one of the miracles that point to its divine authorship. The fact that it agrees with itself is a testament to the author being the Holy Spirit of God.

I grew up before the digital age. We could not imagine having our Bible on our phone. Our phones were connected to the wall of our house or on a table. We used our phones to talk to people who were not in our house. The only information we could gather from our phones was whatever the other person on the line told us.

At that time, our Bibles were books that were on tables or in bookshelves. We would retrieve them from the tables or bookshelves to read them. Most of us could read. The people who could not read (small children, people who did not have their glasses) would rely on others to read for them. Almost everyone that I knew respected the Bible. Some that I knew went so far as to worship the actual book (bibliolatry). They would religiously not let it hit the floor, would never let anything be placed upon it, would sleep with it under their pillow, etc. This treatment of the Bible is extreme and is to be avoided. We are to worship the Lord and serve Him only.

If we want to know the Voice of the Lord, we must know the Bible.

There are at least eight ways we can absorb the Bible into our lives. We can *hear, read, study, memorize, meditate upon, copy, translate and recite the Bible* to put it into our lives. While this list is not exhaustive, it is a good starting point for further consideration.

By the way, **the third tool that God used to communicate who He is, was the life and work of Jesus Christ.** There is much more to come on this later.

A. Hear

The most common way people have gripped the Scripture, down through the centuries, has been to hear the spoken Word. As readers have raised their voices, hearers have been blessed to know that God loves them.

I have often required my students to read the Bible during the school term. Since my students often become leaders in the church, they would do well to master the Bible. Many of them engage their ears in this as they listen to someone read it in their favorite translation.

I do not understand all I know. This is something I know and understand. There is something powerful in the *hearing* of the Word of God. God speaks through His written Word proclaimed by a human voice. The effect is authoritative and alive. The Word of God seems to come alive when a human voice proclaims it. One of the most spine-tingling experiences I have ever had was when a gifted orator or singer recited one or more of the Psalms. Take the time right now to experience this for yourself. I would recommend Psalm 139 recited by Michael W Smith. Find it on YouTube.

B. Read

One of the very best ways to get the Bible into your mind is to crack it open and read it. There is no substitute for this. One of the systems we use in reading is for mileage. We read to get the overall story into our heads. I cannot tell you how many times God's other Voices have used the fruit of this in my own experience. Almost weekly for half century, the Lord has used a Biblical story to say something like, "Your current situation is like the story of…in the Bible." He has used this practice to tell me things that I otherwise would not have known.

He has used this system to shape my life and ministry more times than I can count. He can do this because when I was 11 years old, He convinced me that I needed to start reading His Word. I began reading four chapters a day to read the Bible through once a year. Later, He added six more chapters a day. Every morning, I would read five Psalms to get to know God's heart. (Did I mention

Section 1 The Voice of the Lord

He loves you?) I would then read the Proverb for the day. (There are 31 of them.) I would then continue where I left off the day before in the rest of the Bible.

When I went to my first year of Bible College, I was reading ten chapters a day before I began my official Bible study for school. I am not saying this to brag, just to demonstrate the level of commitment that I had at that time in my life. This practice has led me to know the Voice of the Lord very well. There is no substitute for reading the Word of God. By this practice we can go through the Word of God to get to know the God of the Word. If you are serious about knowing the Voice of the Lord, you will consistently open His book and read it.

C. Study

One of my mentors, the late Dr. Howard Hendricks, used to say that the only book he ever wrote that was worth reading was the one he coauthored with his son. The title was *Living By the Book*. Having read most of his books and having interviewed some of his other students who have read the rest of them, I can honestly say that he was right. He was an amazing teacher. However, his books were not easy to read. The subject of this book was proper Bible study. Since then, Dr. Hendricks (Prof) put some of the material found in that book on YouTube. It may be found if you search for Howard Hendricks, *Living by the Book* video series.[1]

Observation

Observation is the first step in Bible study. In this step, the student of the Bible must ask and answer the question, "What does it say?" One of the most obvious ways we can accomplish this is to

---

[1] Dr. Howard Hendricks - "Living By the Book" video series, Dallas Theological Seminary, YouTube. Accessed Mar. 2024. https://www.youtube.com/watch?v=S55huHC_0_k&list=PLHVLAsJuPfmUeA6eOavI0NheF8Ra0sLu2

1 Scripture

read it. This time, however, we are not reading for mileage. Rather, we are reading the Bible to really understand what it is saying to us. When answering this most basic of questions, it is important to remember some guidelines for proper hermeneutics (a technical word for the science of interpreting texts like the Bible).

First, we need to look for the most obvious meaning of the reading in our native language. The standard goes something like, "When the plain sense makes good sense, look for no other sense for that would be non-sense." Although the *interpretation* proper comes in the next step, some students of the Bible jump the proverbial gun. They look for all kinds of hidden meanings at the *observation* stage in the process. Real hidden meanings (the ones put there by God) are rare in the Bible. He wants us to know Him, remember? Why would He hide meanings in the book that is designed to reveal Him to us? That would make no sense. For this reason, please avoid looking for hidden meanings in the Bible. They are too rare for a casual reader to see.

Since the goal of this first step is to *observe* what the text says, we must begin with the somewhat laborious tasks of textual study. Tools like grammatical construction, word definitions, and the parsing of verbs help us with this. In short, it takes work. I have found that there are very few who are interested in doing the work that it takes to answer the question, "What does it say?" Some of my classmates at the seminary got a wake-up call on this from Professor Hendricks.

About three weeks into my first semester, I began to hear some moaning from my classmates concerning one of "Prof's" assignments. Those of us who had been studying Professor Hendiricks' teaching tactics knew, but were warned not to reveal, what was coming. The students were given an assignment that seemed very difficult to them. They were asked to find twenty-five separate and distinct *observations* in an English translation of Acts 1:8. This is the verse that serves nicely as an outline for the rest of the Book of Acts.

Section 1 The Voice of the Lord

There are about fifteen obvious *observations* in the verse. Most of my peers found these in less than an hour. They then began to discuss some other "*observations*" which ultimately turned out to be *interpretations,* so these were begrudgingly jettisoned from their lists.

Most of my classmates found about five more *observations* and a few more *interpretations* that they included in their list to complete the assignment. All of this was fun to watch, knowing what was going to happen in the next class period. (I found out later that there were one or two students who actually turned in the required 25 *observations*.)

Professor Hendricks instructed the class to hand their paper to the student next to them. (Yes, they used paper back then.) They then read aloud to the class the list that their fellow classmate had handed to them. Amid groans and laughter, various verdicts were handed down from the class on each supposed *observation.* The vast majority of them were judged *interpretations,* rather than *observations.*

Then, that most illustrious of teachers, threw them a major curve. He told them to go back and find 25 more *observations!* You should have heard the moaning after *that* class period. Some of my classmates were livid. They did everything but call down heaven as their witness that this torturous assignment was from the pit of all that is unholy. Some of them were on the verge of dropping the class, so I intervened and encouraged them to just try and do the assignment. By the next class, they were glad they had not quit.

The big reveal came in the next class session. After letting them squirm for a quarter of an hour, Prof could stand it no longer. He told them that he had, at that moment, twenty-six hundred separate and distinct *observations* from that one verse. He had saved these from students' discoveries over the past several decades. Think of it, 2,600 *observations* on one verse. I have been informed that he went on to collect about a thousand more before his death. It is probably safe to say that this is the most studied verse in the Bible!

Sadly, most students of the Bible skip this step entirely. They spend woefully too little time and effort answering the question, "What does it say?" If they would spend more time on this *observation* step, they would hit the mark more often. Remember, there can and should be many *observations* discovered in any Biblical text, the more understanding here, the less misunderstanding later.

Interpretation

The second step in Biblical hermeneutics is *interpretation* proper. This is where the student of the Bible asks and answers the question, "What does it mean?" There is no wiggle room at this point. Answering this wrong can mean disaster. Missing this mark can bring damnation for many. One of the reasons that the first family of our race (Adam and Eve) cast all of us into sin was Eve's misunderstanding that she could not even *touch* the tree. Cults have been started when leaders mistake the meaning of a text. Just so we are clear, there is only **one** *interpretation* of a text. The only exception to this rule is when the Bible says there is more than one meaning. This, as I have already stated, is very rare.

Because the Bible is the first and most objective of all the Lord's Voices, **the *observation* step cannot be overemphasized.** A casual, or even devotional reading of the Bible is not enough to *interpret* it. If we do not understand the Bible, how can we know that we hear God's Voice? Many missteps in following the Lord Jesus Christ begin at this point. For this reason, it is vital that the follower of Christ become an *observant* student of God's written Word. **Please** begin to make time to dig into the normal grammatical text and *observe* what the Bible says **before** you *interpret* it.

When we look for *observations* about a passage, we look for as many as we can find, in the hopes that we may be able to discover the one, real meaning (*interpretation*). As a rule, the more observations (not *interpretations*) we can find in step one, the more likely we are to be confident that we have arrived at the correct

Section 1 The Voice of the Lord

interpretation of that passage (step two). The closer we come to this, the closer we may be able *interpret* what God is trying to say to us.

The requirement is very simple. We must understand what the original readers of the text understood when they read it. While this sounds easy, it is quite involved. The student of the Bible must move back in time, beyond linguistic boundaries and past cultural barriers to get to the heart of the message that the original audience received. Some have spent their entire professional lives making this possible for the rest of us. We would do well to know who these stalwart students were and use their knowledge.

The next part of this step is that of synthesis. We take our work of *interpreting* the parts and restate the whole in our own words. Once we have done the homework, we are probably qualified to produce our own version of the passage. Keep in mind that we should judiciously use the homework of former Bible students.

The reason it is vital that you rewrite the passage in your own words is because you are living in your own culture. You have your own language, and you live in your own time. You are perfectly unique. God wants you, that unique person, to know Him intimately.

You are a person that piqued God's interest thousands of years before He made you. When sin entered the picture, the odds of you knowing God became extremely long. Most people down through the annals of time have not known God at all. They became enemies of God and feared Him. All of us have been born into this kind of adversarial relationship with God.

Once you go through the hard work of *interpreting* a passage, you shorten the odds of knowing God considerably. When you take the next step of putting the passage into your own words, the connection becomes palpable. The greatest joy I have ever experienced has happened after I peeled back the last layer of understanding in a passage: I found God ready with a warm embrace for this kid who made it all the way to Him. This fantastic scene has played out many times in my life. It is my sincere hope that you experience it too.

Application

There are three, not two steps in studying the Word of God. The third step is just as important as the other two. Sadly, however, many who study the Bible seem content to stop before *applying* the passage. We must never forget that one of the most clearly warned sins is hearing what God says and not obeying Him. This was the foolish builder who Jesus described at the end of the Sermon on the Mount. That builder's end was tragic, indeed.

After we do the work of understanding what the Bible says (observation) and what it means (interpretation), we need to find out how the Lord wants us to *apply* it to our lives. In the *application* stage of Biblical interpretation, we need to ask and answer the question, "What does this passage mean for (or to) me?" "How should I put this passage into my context?" While there should be many *observations* drawn from a passage, and one *interpretation* of that passage, there can be infinitely more *applications* of that passage.

For more help on this step, I encourage you to visit Dr. Howard Hendricks' YouTube channel.[2] He explained the specifics of the *application* step in this video.[3] I see no reason to reinvent the proverbial wheel when Professor Hendricks did such a good job of explaining it. I would encourage you to go through the various videos, in order, slowly, taking time out to really press into the assignments as Prof directs. Just do what he tells you to do, and his excellent teaching will bless you from beyond his grave.

---

2   Ibid.
3   Living by The Book - Application - Session 1, gracebibleonline. Accessed Mar. 2024. https://www.youtube.com/watch?v=HFpoGuVsHXY&list=PLY23PoCP4_jsFx6LOPm4WCK2T3ITXOoFB&index=16

Section 1 The Voice of the Lord

D. Memorize

I was encouraged as a boy to hide the Word of God in my heart. Even now, the Father regularly uses those passages to guide me. He takes the Bible that I have internalized and applies the stories to whatever I am facing. The Lord can speak into the lives of His children when they have memorized passages of the Bible for Him to access. If you want the Lord to speak to you about tomorrow, plant material from His Bible in your heart today. Seek Him in this way and see how He blesses you.

E. Meditate

This is one of the most misunderstood ways that the Lord has ordained for us to handle His Word. When we hear the word, "meditate," we typically get a picture in our heads of a Tibetan monk, humming some incomprehensible mantra, trying to obtain the emptiness that brings oneness with the universe. Biblical meditation does not look like this at all. It is quite simple in reality. Once we have hidden God's Word in our heart through memorization, we should think about it. The idea behind meditation is that of a cow chewing her cud.

I have no experience as a farmer, nor am I someone who knows cows. I *have* learned, however, that cows have certain habits. Cows have four stomachs. They use these stomachs, in succession, to digest their food. They can stand or lie down in a field for a long time just chewing. This is called chewing the cud.

When they eat the grass from the ground, it goes into their first stomach. Later, they cough up (I think the technical term for this is hoyp) the contents of this stomach into their mouths in order to chew their food some more. When they swallow this, it goes

1 Scripture

into their second stomach, and so on, until they have fully digested what they have eaten.

In the same way, we need to chew on the passages of Scripture that we have memorized. We should bring them up to chew. We should prayerfully mumble the Word of God back to Him. This mumbling takes the form of questions or restatements so that we can fully grasp what God wants to say to us. I have found that the insights of meditation are much more impactful than any other method of internalizing the Bible. When we meditate on the Word of God, we are translating the Bible. This translation is written in our most intimate heart language. It takes time and prolonged effort to really press into this. However, the payoff is phenomenal.

F. Copy

In the old days, there were no laser printers, nor were there any copy machines, not even a dot matrix was available to copy pages. There were not any typewriters or self-contained ink pens either. All they had was something sharp (a quill) to dip into the ink and something on which to write (papyrus). Scribes were the people who copied things. When copying something as precious as the Word of God, they had systems in place to ensure that the new copy was an exact image of the old copy.

One way to put the Word of God into our lives is to copy our own set of the canonized 66 books of the Bible. When a king was about to ascend the throne in Israel, one requirement was for him to write himself a copy of the Law (Pentateuch or first five books of the Bible) (Deut. 17:18). There is no record of this taking place in the history of the kings. However, we are called to be kings and priests in a lost and dying world, could this command be for us?

Section 1 The Voice of the Lord

G. Translate

One of the ongoing battles of the church age is about Biblical translations. Back when Jesus walked the earth, most of the Bible was written in Hebrew. The problem was that very few people spoke that language. What they spoke was Aramaic and/or Greek. This included the people that God called His own, the Jews. To remedy this, seventy Biblical scholars got together and wrote what we now know as the Septuagint (Seventy). The Septuagint was the most accepted Greek translation of the Old Testament. Whenever you see the Roman numeral for 70 (LXX) you should know that this is referring to the Greek translation of the Old Testament.

There were some purists, however, that thought the original Hebrew was all the Lord would allow. They fought tooth and nail to keep the Septuagint translation from gaining popularity. In the end, it was a rival faction that led to the end of the Jewish use of the LXX. When Christians began utilizing it as their main source of information concerning the Old Testament, the Jews largely abandoned it (in the second century A.D.).

A man named Jerome instigated the next stage in the development of this idea of *lingua franca* or the language of the people. He realized that Greek was no longer the language of the people and that people had to attend special studies in Greek to read their Bibles. Jerome answered this problem by translating the Bible into the language that the people spoke, Latin. This language was called Vulgar, and this term became the title for the new translation, the Vulgate.

The Vulgate was used as the translation of choice for about a thousand years. This soon became a problem for the average person. Over time, the average person began to speak a variety of other languages. Members of the clergy were the only people who spoke the language of the Bible. Latin became the intellectual, holy language. Men would study Latin so that they could converse with

1 Scripture

other educated men who spoke other languages. All church services were held in Latin, and the only reliable Bibles were in this language. The people did not have Bibles in their own language. Attempts were made to remedy this situation, most of which were violently ended.

In 1611, a fellow named King James commissioned some Godly, Biblical scholars to write the Bible in English. This translation of the Bible became known as the King James Version. As what was seen later as a marketing ploy, the King put his stamp of approval on it and called it the Authorized Version. It was originally called this so that more people would buy and read it. The question of who authorized it has been a hot debate ever since. Some have contested that it was really authorized by God. However, they have no evidence to back up this claim.

This debate brings up a very important point as to the standard upon which we base judgments with respect to Biblical accuracy. The King James Version is a translation of the Bible that was for the people of England in 1611. The marketing ploy aside, this translation was never meant to be the standard for all other translations. The real standard to which all versions or translations should bow the knee is that of the Autographs. The Autographs are the actual books or letters that the Biblical authors wrote with their own hands.

The problem with the Autographs being the true authority is that we do not have the actual letters or books that the Biblical authors wrote. We have copies of the Autographs. To be more precise, we have copies of copies, many generations of copies from the Autographs. As with any copies of copies, the farther removed from the Autograph (the original), the more corrupt the copy.

The term Lower Textual Criticism addresses this problem. Lower Textual Criticism is the science that says that we need to get as close to the Autographs as possible. With modern archeology

Section 1 The Voice of the Lord

and other related disciplines, we have been able to get very close to many Autographs. With one of the Gospels, we have actually been able to get within two copies of the Autograph (parts of the Gospel of John).

Since the standard is to get as close to the Autograph as possible, the newer translations have gone further back in time, archeologically speaking. These are written in modern languages that people are speaking now, as well. We now have translations that are in the language of the people and are closer to the Autographs.

The real power in a translation of the Bible is that of confidence. When I was learning Greek several decades ago, I found that the verses I was translating kept sounding familiar. When I would later look up the verse in a modern translation, I found that I had translated the verses almost word for word from the original Greek into my *lingua franca*.

This helped me to know with confidence that I was competent to take the Greek and make it understandable. The version that I was using was God's Word for me and my culture. Again, this is another case in which the work that I put in at the front end paid off in the end. If you have the time to spend studying Hebrew or Greek, I encourage you to do so. If not, there are many time-tested tools that are designed to help in word studies and other translation functions. One very helpful tool is the Blue Letter Bible site on the Internet.

H. Recite

Once you have hidden the Word of God in your heart, you should begin to allow the Holy Spirit to guide you into where to insert it into your day. *"A word fitly spoken and in due season is like apples of gold in settings of silver."* (Proverbs 25:11 AMPC). You can

1 Scripture

speak God's Word into situations that desperately need them. The only requirement is for the Word of God to be in your heart in the first place. Memorization of the Bible is a prerequisite for recitation.

2
Saints

Those whom we know are hearing and following the Voice of the Lord

I would like to say that all my wild plans have been successful. However, I am trying to write a book that is at least truthful. I have dragged my poor wife and family all over the United States, following the Voice of the Lord as I thought I heard it. About eight years into our marriage, I asked my bride to make one "last move" with me. This was the one that I was sure was from Him. Looking back, all the moves had benefits; they caused us to be the people the Lord can use today. However, this one was probably the one that caused me to be the most useful with respect to my current ministry.

2 Saints

In 1995, we left Dallas Theological Seminary and moved to a very small town in southern West Virginia. This was the first time I decided to leave the ministry. I felt the leading of the Lord to work with my hands; to live a quiet, peaceful life as we raised our three children. Sixteen years later, we left there, two children richer and inestimably wiser. The main reason for this wisdom was found in my choice to submit to godly authority. This is one lesson that everyone needs to learn. Few of us are interested in the humility that it takes to learn it.

Shortly after I arrived as God's gift to those poor, backwoods country folk, I found that they were God's gift to me. Dallas Seminary had taught me to highly esteem the Bible; these gentle folks taught me that other saints (people) were needed to properly follow the Lord. As we learn to submit ourselves to others in the body of Christ, we become what He wants us to be. I arrived arrogantly ambitious; we left quietly confident—in the Lord.

The key to this transformation was my decision to fully submit to three godly men who were elders in the congregation we were attending. They were each about a decade older than me; yet light-years wiser. I quickly devised my golden rule of engagement for them. If one of them casually mentioned some activity that might be nice for me to do or not do, I was to consider this as a direct command from the Lord. One of these men, for example, mentioned that a home improvement store was hiring and that I might be good in this line of work. A week later, I began a 14-year business relationship with that organization. I was serious about finding the Voice of the Lord as He spoke through the mouths of His saints.

The best way to identify which saint to listen to is to ask God. This is a prayer that is like asking for wisdom. The idea is that the Lord will give you wisdom in finding this person. This person, in turn, will give you wisdom in hearing the Lord's Voice. It may seem like circular reasoning. However, I assure you that it is not.

Section 1 The Voice of the Lord

Asking the Lord to provide a person who can direct you in this way is honoring the Lord and His church. What you are saying when you ask God for such a person is that you do not put trust in yourself or your ability to reason things out. Rather, that you trust God to send His spokesperson into your life.

My relationship with those gracious men eventually ended for me just as it began. One day the Lord clearly told me to exit their ranks. God confirmed this directive many times before I listened and obeyed Him. I needed these multiple confirmations because those men had been very helpful to me for seven years. During that time, they went so far as to welcome me into their ranks as a fellow elder. After I left, I began to see how many others in the body of Christ were floundering in their journeys with Christ because they did not have a foundation of being under authority. I do not feel that all of us should stay under the same spiritual authority. This is because there are inherent abuses associated with this kind of power. However, all of us should spend some time under authority to better learn the Voice of the Lord.

How Do We Leverage Saints into Voice Meters?

One of the most intriguing stories in the Bible on this subject is that of the calling of the last Old Testament Judge, Samuel. Samuel was a boy who was being raised in the Tabernacle by the old priest, Eli (I Samuel 3). One night, God called to Samuel. Young Samuel thought Eli was calling him, so he ran to the old priest and answered him. Eli sent him back to bed, as any good guardian would do with a child who seemingly does not want to go to sleep. This happened three times before Eli realized that the Lord was calling to Samuel. He instructed the young prophet what to say to hear the Lord. Thus Samuel began a long ministry of hearing and obeying the Voice of the Lord.

There are several principles that are noteworthy from this story. First, the Voice the Lord utilized was that of an authority figure in Samuel's upbringing. Eli was not calling Samuel, but the Voice sounded like Eli to Samuel. The Lord has used my earthly father's voice for many decades. He calls me "Tommy," just as my father did when he was alive. If the person who raised you did not abuse you as a child, you should expect this to be a Voice that the Lord might try with you. I believe that the Lord may try many Voices until you learn to recognize His.

Second, the authority figure recognized that the Lord was trying to talk to the young one and instructed him on what to do. Jesus did something similar in Matthew 16 when He responded to Peter's declaration concerning Christ's identity. After Peter declared that Jesus was the Christ, Jesus told him, and the other disciples, that the Holy Spirit was the source of that information. He was telling Peter that this was what the Holy Spirit sounded like. This tidbit was going to prove to be invaluable for Peter in the coming years.

Third, Jesus (and possibly Eli) knew the vital urgency associated with finding and developing the next generation of spiritual leaders. It is not enough to be concerned with our own personal ministries. Leaders must be obsessed with what will happen after our time has passed. **If you are a Christian leader on any level, your overwhelming passion should be to reproduce yourself in the lives of many other young leaders for the coming generations.**

Very early in my training for ministry (I was 11 years old), one of my mentors etched on my heart the need to be more excited about what *others* were doing than about what *I* was doing. This was presented to me as one strategy for motivating others for Christian service. I learned this principle of motivation so completely that after several decades of ministry, I can honestly say that my personal "ministry" receives very little of my attention.

Almost all of my energy goes to what others are doing. The thing I get the most excited about is when I hear something said by

Section 1 The Voice of the Lord

one of my students that came directly from the Lord. I also begin to shout when the Spirit tells me that He told someone to do or say something. I make it a point to communicate this to the individual with a word about the need to follow this Voice in the future. I think Peter was able to do what he did in the New Testament based on Jesus' encouragement on that day (Matthew 16).

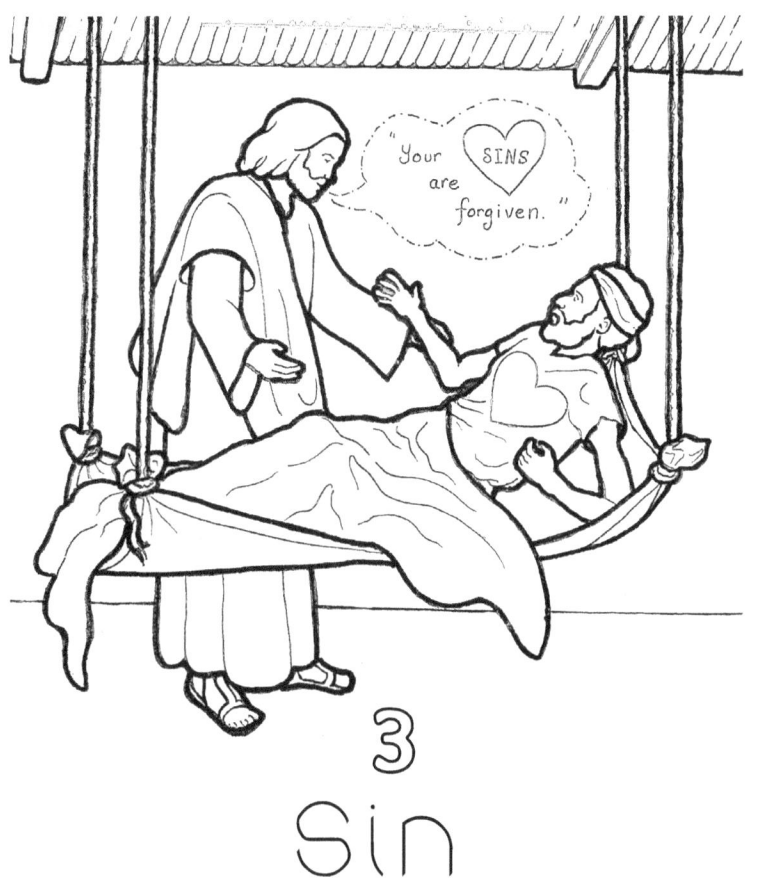

3
Sin

The conviction, cost, and forgiveness of sin is God's clearest Voice

One of the most obvious needs we have is to discard sin. This is an especially sad circumstance given another fact—that sin is always with us. When we are not the instigators of it, we are certainly and consistently the victims of it. It is on both sides of this scandalous equation that the Lord has chosen to find us. Through sin, the Lord has allowed us to learn His amazing Voice. If we seek Him with all our hearts, He can be heard even in the thing that scars us most, sin.

Section 1 The Voice of the Lord

Conviction

It has been well said that the Lord loves us completely just the way we are. (Hey, have you heard that God loves you?) He also loves us enough that He does not want us to stay there. **God loves you!** He sent His Son to die on a cross to save you. Once you accept this free gift of life, you are absolutely forgiven for every sin—past, present and future. Your sin is behind you, but there is a process to keep it there. In I John 1:9 we read that as the children of God, if we confess our sin, He is faithful and just to forgive our sin and clean us up. The question is, how do we know that we have sinned?

In the 16th chapter of the Gospel of John, Jesus told His disciples of One who would come after Him. This One would come after Jesus ascended. We know this One as the Holy Spirit. The Holy Spirit has many roles. One of these is to convict the world of sin.

The Holy Spirit convicts those who sin. This means that God speaks to sinners. This is the *most obvious* Voice of the Lord. **That Voice, in the back of your head, that tells you that you have done wrong is not some nagging throwback to bygone eras of unenlightened cultures, but the actual Voice of Almighty God.** To say otherwise is foolish indeed. I am not referring to the false voice of accusation that the enemy employs, but the clear, specific, authoritative utterance, *"That was wrong."*

The Lord does not want the rebuking of you to go unheard. He can and does utilize this Voice very often. All you need to do is recognize this Voice when the Holy Spirit speaks. **Remember, the goal is for you to learn what God sounds like.** One way I practice this is to ask Him what He wants me *to do* about my particular sin that He has called out. I confess that He is true (about the fact that I have sinned), and then I ask Him what He wants me to do about it. I listen. He often tells me to go to particular individuals and confess my sin to them, as well. This is a good practice when trying

3 Sin

to learn what He sounds like. **By the way, if you want to hear Him speak again, do what He says.**

Forgiveness

One of the most influential of the Voices that the Lord uses is that of forgiveness. He has wrapped up some overwhelming and unmistakable emotions with this one. It may be correctly said that the specific persons of the Godhead have forgiven us all at some crucial times in history. At these times, they were deeply moved with emotions. When we act like God in forgiveness, the Lord connects with us at such a deep level that we are forever marked.

With Christ in John 13 and 14

One of the bluntest discussions in the ministry of Christ was during the upper room discourse. Having very little time left with the disciples, Jesus did not mince words in this meeting. He was very direct. One thing He said was that all of them would fall away from following Him. They predictably denied that this would happen, and one of them even promised on oath that he would not.

Section 1 The Voice of the Lord

Luke 22:61 tells us that at the moment the cock crowed, right after Peter's third denial of Jesus, Jesus turned and looked through the crowd and found Peter's eyes. *O, the depths of betrayal Christ must have felt at that moment!* One of His disciples had betrayed Him with a kiss, and this one called down curses to put distance between Jesus and him.

If any of us had experienced this level of betrayal, there would be more than words between us at our next meeting. However, Jesus did not condemn Peter when they next spoke. Instead, He continued Peter's installation as a leader of the new church. The only allusion to Peter's thrice denial was Jesus asking a probing question three times (John 21). During or sometime after the shock of looking at Peter's guilty face on the night of His betrayal, Jesus forgave him. It might have happened during that gut-wrenching time when He was bearing the punishment for all sin.

The Horrific Cost Required for Sin on the Cross

Since Jesus was the God-Man, there is an obvious question concerning how God could die. There is a well-known and established theological fact: gods cannot die. The one true God is no exception. There is no wiggle room on this point. This would be the first and most compelling reason for saying that Jesus could not have died on a cross. **Since God cannot die, how could Jesus die?** Unless He was something less than God, He could not die. Despite this impossibility, Jesus is God and He did die. This would be the epitome of impossibilities by itself, however, *there is more.*

Why did He have to die this kind of death? He could have died of natural causes, or of some disease. However, He died as a condemned criminal. Dying is bad enough. Did He really need to suffer the shame of a mock trial and a public execution? As if this was not bad enough, *there is more*.

Jesus died the most public and humiliating way the cruelty of humankind has devised. It is one thing to be killed in front of a huge crowd, it is quite another for the condemned person to draw the crowd by publicly carrying His tool of execution (the Cross) through the city to advertise the event.

Crucifixion had the added humiliation of lasting for a very long time. There are cases of this form of punishment lasting for days. Days of onlookers seeing the most intimate details of the condemned person's agony in the throes of death. All of this was happening while He was naked; His body exposed to the cruelty of that crowd and the soldiers. This was not yet the ultimate cruelty that Jesus endured.

As He stood on the Cross in an agonizing posture, He said some things and then cried out in a loud voice that it was finished. Then the Gospel writers record that He gave up the ghost and died. The question is, **"What made Him die?"** Modern medical professionals have informed us that death by crucifixion is not only very painful, but also specific in its mechanism. It is this mechanism that is a most curious impossibility. The mechanism of death in crucifixion is suffocation, or rather, asphyxiation.

The way a person usually died on a cross was by a lack of oxygen in the blood. This was due to the victim's inability to breathe. This inability was due to loss of strength in the legs from exhaustion or blood loss. The victim was stretched out on the cross so that he would need to stand up on legs whose feet were nailed to a board. This would be required to breathe. After hours or days of this cycle (standing on injured feet, taking a few breaths, becoming weak enough to need to rest with the arms holding the victim's weight, then not being able to breathe), the victim would fall asleep or unconscious. Death would come because the lungs would be

Section 1 The Voice of the Lord

unable to inflate. This was due to the arms holding up the body of the victim and not letting the muscles surrounding the ribs to expand the ribs for inhalation.

A mechanism of death is required. There must be something that kills a person even if the person kills himself. This, however, was not so in the case of Christ's death. **He was supposed to die of suffocation or the lack of the ability to breathe effectively. However, just prior to His death, He cried out in a loud voice. This was not the way people died on crosses. They died quietly.** It takes breath to speak. This fact was echoed by the actions of the soldiers who were guarding Him. They broke the legs of the other two victims so that they could not push up on their legs. This would have effectively ended their suffering, because they would not have been able to get another breath.

When they came to Jesus, they saw that He was already dead. This surprised them so they poked His heart with a spear, just to make sure. What came out was a good description of coagulated blood. This was an indisputable sign to those professional executioners (Roman soldiers) and to us that He had already been dead.

He died for our sins. Let's take a moment for me to illustrate the punishment for sin. It gives weight to what Jesus suffered. During the first Gulf War, Saddam Hussein had his retreating army set fire to the oil wells in Kuwait. These were supposed to serve as effective smoke screens to slow the coalition's advance against him. News agencies calculated that it would take a very long time for someone to put out those fires. As history recorded, however, it took a bunch of Texas Wildcatters only a few months to bring them under control.

Those oil fires were like flame-throwers that were about six feet around, throwing powerful jets of fire about a hundred feet into the air. It is not possible for a body to survive it, but a heavily suited board and surfer could conceivably ride on one of those oil fires for a stunt. The force of the fire could easily hold up the weight of a person. It is interesting that the place reserved for the enemies of God is called the lake of fire. The idea behind this description was that a person would be swimming in fire for all eternity.

Let us continue to propose that this oil fire, if it could last for all eternity future, would be the punishment for one sin. People, like me, would have racked up the punishment for their many sins to a fireball the size of the Sun. If we combine the sins of all the people who have ever lived, the punishment for all these sins must have filled the universe with the fire and wrath of the Almighty, Holy God. Jesus suffered horrifically for that punishment.

What Killed Him?

Since there is no question that Jesus was dead, the question remains, what killed Him? While it would be foolish to try to calculate all the interactions within the Godhead, there are some clues that may help:

First, Jesus told His disciples that He would freely lay down His life and that He would take it up again. This fact puts to rest the dilemma concerning which people group physically killed the Christ. There is no room for the charge of "Christ Killer" to ever be laid at the feet of the Jews. The Romans also did not kill Jesus. These two people groups put Jesus on a cross, but that did not kill Him.

There is another issue that is forever settled by Jesus' power in this arena. Because Jesus could predict this historic event before its occurrence, it follows that He had at least a modicum of control over the details of the event itself. He was not taken by surprise by a band of thugs. They certainly were a band of thugs. However, He was fully in control. The best evidence of this is found at His arrest.

In chapter 18 of his Gospel, the apostle John recorded the most unusual manner that Jesus was apprehended. After establishing that it was Jesus that they sought, Jesus uttered the words, "I

Section 1 The Voice of the Lord

am He" to His would-be captors. At this, they all fell backwards. This was a remarkable reaction given the fact that they came to arrest Him, armed to the teeth, with numbers on their side. At the word of Jesus, they meekly fell backward! They had to recover from this stunned state to actually take Christ into custody. They were not in control of this situation, He was.

Second, He became the essence of sin. He became sin, Who knew no sin, that we might become the righteousness of Christ. (See II Cor. 5:21.) He became fully engulfed in the penalty of our sin, without ever having participated in sin. In the thinking of us sinners, He got none of the fun, and took all the beating.

Third, God cannot look upon sin. This does not detract from His Omniscience (God is all-knowing) or His Omnipresence (God is everywhere). This is a choice that is based on His holiness. He is totally separated from any hint of sin.

There is an interesting side note at this point found in the disposition of sin and a sinful vessel. When humans encounter disease, we can catch it. The same can be said of the sin that we encounter. It usually, apart from the work of the Holy Spirit, drags us down. However, God is far from being like us. He cannot look at or be in the presence of sin or a sinful vessel because He destroys it. Sin does not impact the Holiness of God; God wipes sin out of existence.

For this reason, God could not look at or be in the presence of Jesus Christ at the moment when He became the shameful, ugliness of human sin. Since God could have nothing to do with sin, Christ's becoming the expression of human sin must have violently repulsed the Father.

Fourth, the Father turned His face away from Christ. This must have been the ultimate counterpoint in history. For all of eternity past, the triune God had been together, and then God split. Jesus took your sin and mine knowing that this would

3 Sin

happen. This was probably the cup that Jesus was referring to when He asked three times for it to be removed. It is no wonder that Jesus sweat great drops of blood in the garden.

There is a telling ***silence*** that permeates the story of the death of Jesus.

When He was falsely accused of many crimes in three illegal trials, His response was *silence*.

When the leaders of the Jews mocked and beat Him, *silence*.

When He was mocked and beaten by the much more efficient and cruel Roman soldiers, *silence*.

When they stripped Him and paraded Him through the city streets, *silence*.

When He fell under the load of the Cross that He was forced to carry, *silence*.

When His hands and feet were nailed to the wood, *silence*.

When He hung there, stripped and bleeding for all to see, *silence*.

Section 1 The Voice of the Lord

When the crowd teased Him and goaded Him to come down from the Cross, *silence*.

When the soldiers cast lots for the robe that they had stolen from Him, *silence*.

As He was forced to pull against the burning nails in His hands and feet to get a breath of air, *silence*.

But when the Father turned away for the first time in eternity, He cried out, "MY GOD, MY GOD, WHY HAVE YOU FORSAKEN ME!?"

No wonder He cried out that He was thirsty. No wonder He cried out in agony that His Father had forsaken Him. No wonder there was darkness on the land in the middle of the day for three hours. It was as though the Father was saying to us, "I will not look at my Son in our cosmic agony. You will not see Him either!"

At that moment, the God part of the God-Man must have been ripped away; all the torment for all the punishment for all the sins of all mankind for all of time was crammed into the open wound. There is no description in any language that can even start to plumb the depths of the unadulterated agony and desolation felt by Jesus. No wonder He gave up the ghost and died. **The question is forever settled concerning who killed Jesus. WE DID.**

I am rather frightened when I think about the depth of depravity to which people are capable of sinking. Your sin scares me. The thought of your sin keeps me on my proverbial toes. However, the thing that really terrifies me and causes me a great deal of fear and trembling is the depth of depravity to which I am able to stoop. *My sin put Christ on the Cross and kept Him there until He gave up the ghost and died.* This is the attitude all of us should adopt.

I am beginning to believe that when Jesus cried out for the Father to forgive them, He was responding to the heart of the Father. At that moment, the Father may have been reaching down to grab the earth between His Almighty fingers and squash us out of existence. When Jesus asked the Father to forgive us, God may have uttered something like, "Fine, but they will not look at You a moment longer in Your suffering." And He turned out the lights for about three hours.

God Completely Connects with Fellow Forgivers.

As we discussed earlier, there are two ways that the Lord connects with us in this Voice (sin). The Holy Spirit convicts us of specific sin in our lives, which is the first half of this Voice. The second half is that of a strong, yet mystically emotional connection that the Father has with those who actively forgive others. This is the forgiveness that acknowledges the sin that someone has done against us and then allows the grace of God to remove the desire for revenge.

When Jesus asked the Father to forgive us for all that we were doing to Him while He was hanging on the Cross, God must have done so; we are still here. Jeremiah informed us that it is because of the Lord's great love that we are not consumed (Lamentations 3:23). I cannot imagine a moment when God withheld our destruction more intensely than at that moment. As I said before, instead of obliterating us, He settled for turning the lights out for about three hours.

With respect to the Voice of the Lord, I believe that the Father has a special place in His heart for those who follow Him in really forgiving from their hearts. **It is as though He considers us part of His divine posse of forgivers, extending His forgiveness to a lost and dying world.** When we forgive in this way, it is like we are His favorites. He actually likes people who forgive, as close personal friends. In case anyone doubts me, check what Jesus had to say on this in Matthew 6, just after He gave the teaching on prayer.

4
Suffering

As the ultimate therapist, God intervenes in our suffering with His Presence, Power, Purpose, and the Pacifier of His comforting Word

David was once in a tight place. His own king had put a price on his head and he was running for his life. One day he got the bright idea to run to his enemies for safety. The problem with this plan was that they recognized him. Being the clever fellow that he was, he pretended to be insane when they brought him to their king. The king was not amused. He ordered David out of his presence and thereby spared David's life.

4 Suffering

Apparently after he was out of danger from those enemies, he wrote Psalm 34.

This Psalm is dedicated to those who suffer. David reminded his children that the Lord is a person they can run to for safety when suffering times are upon them. This Psalm may rightly be extended to us. When we encounter hardship and suffering of various kinds, we can be sure that the Lord is our help and refuge. One little verse jumped out at me several years ago. There are very few verses like it in the whole Bible.

In verse 18, David penned these words, *"The LORD is close to the brokenhearted and saves those who are crushed in spirit."* This verse is uncommon because of the placement of the words "the LORD." There are a multitude of passages that admonish God's people to draw near to God in some way. We are directed to come to *Him* for a variety of reasons. However, it seems that one of the main reasons God comes close to *us* is to comfort us in our suffering. When you are in despair, look for God to come close to you with an indescribable comfort.

One of the most tragic stories in the Bible is that of Isaiah. He had a prestigious upbringing, and an impressive education with a seldom-rivaled pedigree. However, God called him to a ministry that would begin and end in frustration and misery. God called him to be ever reaching out in the Name of the Lord to a people who would not listen. He would spend his life writing eloquently, knowing that his words would be seldom read, and largely disregarded by his intended audience. In one of the more notable diatribes, Isaiah reminded his scant readership that they would not listen to or heed his words, that this would bring the judgment of the Lord, which in turn would cause them to cry out to the Lord in their suffering. The Lord would hear their cry for mercy and relieve their suffering. In the middle of this storyline, the prophet threw a verse into the mix that is of great comfort to me.

In Isaiah 30 verse 21, we can read that God has a place with the suffering person. The prophet informed us that God is behind

Section 1 The Voice of the Lord

the sufferer, whispering in his or her ear. Think of it, the only person who really can do anything about our suffering is close enough to you that He can whisper and you can hear Him. If He simply recited the ABC's in my ear, I could find boundless comfort.

There is a ministry that I am finding a new appreciation for among those that I encourage. It is the ministry of presence. Sometimes, all we can do for a person when they are suffering is to be with them. When Job's counselors came to him after his enormous losses, they sat with him for a week. They did not say anything to him in this initial encounter; they just sat with him. It has been rightly surmised that they did right and did not sin in this. It was only when they opened their mouths that they began to chew their proverbial sandals.

This ministry of presence is so widely known that it has become a standard practice among crisis counselors. True to form, God is way ahead of us in our crisis counseling best practices. He has been in the business of comfort for a very long time. What He communicates in our suffering is so far above what we can imagine, that it blows my mind to think of it. In fact, there are really no words that are adequate to describe what God communicates to the person who is suffering and listening.

In the first chapter of the second letter to the Corinthians, the apostle Paul spoke of this and seemed to get his tongue tied. In five verses, Paul repeated one word ten times. I am hard pressed to find a similar passage in the entire Bible. The word that he repeated in its various forms was comfort.

The idea is that God Himself comforts us in our suffering. Part of that comfort comes in Him being close to us, as I mentioned already. Another aspect of the comfort that He brings is that of actual relief from the circumstances of our suffering. It is truly awe-inspiring to watch Him at work on our behalf when we place ourselves in His hands, instead of trying to escape our suffering. His actions, along with His timing, are profoundly on target—every time.

4 Suffering

Even though the Lord can comfort us in these ways, there is another way that is not often discussed in polite circles. It is unthinkable to most, and may be a reason why many will never read this book. Sometimes, our loving heavenly Father chooses to keep us in our suffering state. From our perspective, this is the worst-case scenario. This means that the Lord will not be rescuing us from our suffering any time soon.

It is at this point that I must confess that I have been many places and have seen many things. I am not saying this as some sort of boast, because I do not consider this as a part of who I am. I am writing this to say that of all the pleasures and experiences I have had, there is one experience that is totally unmatched. It is the experience of hearing the Lord speak words of comfort to me. This is pure joy, unmixed or diminished, unspeakable and full of glory.

I love the Word of God for yet another reason. It reminds me that all people are frail and flawed.

The apostle Paul was having a really bad day. He had spent years serving the Lord in various capacities all around the known world. He had suffered persecution in these places and had the marks of the Gospel on his body. He had come back to his base, Jerusalem, for rest and to quietly worship the Lord in fulfilling some vows. It was at this point that his enemies recognized him.

We pick up the story in the 23rd chapter of the book of Acts. After being identified by those who would have his head (literally), Paul had to make two defenses for his behavior as an ambassador for Jesus Christ. His enemies' response was to begin to try to pull him in pieces (again, literally). In the evening, after Roman soldiers rescued him from them and had him under guard, the Lord stepped on the scene and brought the four aspects of comfort to Paul. These were Presence, Power, Purpose, and the amazing Pacifier of His Voice.

We are told in verse 11 that the Lord moved in close to Paul that night. The exact word that Dr. Luke used was "stood." The Lord stood next to Paul. In the letter to the Hebrews, the writer

Section 1 The Voice of the Lord

described the last movement of the Lord Jesus as having sat down at the right hand of God (Hebrews 10:12). Despite this, Luke recorded Jesus as standing in this passage and another one in Acts. The other one is at the stoning of Stephen. It is interesting that Paul (Saul) is present in both instances. What is also interesting is that Paul and Stephen were suffering. It is as though Jesus got up from His rightful place of authority, seated at the right hand of God, to move in close to His suffering servants. He was practicing the ministry of Presence.

The second part of His comfort to the apostle Paul was that of Power. On the night that this took place, Paul was in an army barracks. He had been taken into custody and was surrounded by a company of soldiers. There was undoubtedly an armed guard. Those particular barracks were renown as secure from outside incursion. The Lord Jesus Christ showed His power over the situation just by being there, uninvited.

It was at this point that we can see the third part of the comfort quadrille, that of Purpose. One way that the Lord comforts those who are suffering is by assigning purpose to the suffering. Jesus was comforted as He endured the suffering of His death on the Cross because He could see past the suffering to us, the people that He redeemed from sin (Hebrews 12:2). Jesus (and we) has/have this ministry of reconciliation that comes with a price, suffering (II Corinthians 5:4, 14-15, 18).

The purpose that Jesus gave Paul on that night was that of preaching to the emperor of Rome. This was a big purpose. And, just like every other plan of God that is big, it carried a big price. The Biblical principle is this, the bigger the vision, the greater the suffering that will be required from the servant who carries it out. **The bigger the potential impact, the bigger the required sacrifice.** We must learn to look not at our suffering, but at the reward that our service will produce. That reward is souls won for the Kingdom. And it is well worth it.

4 Suffering

The final part of the comfort juggernaut is that of the Divine Pacifier. This Pacifier may take many forms, but it is essentially the grace of God. Most often, in my hour of need, it takes the form of comforting words. The Lord whispers things like: "I am with you." "Do not fear." "Do not worry, I've got this." "This is from Me, do not struggle." Just as a tiny child finds comfort in a blanket or a furry teddy bear, so the divine words of comfort calm us when we are in turmoil.

How it works is above my pay grade. However, I have begun to look for Him to bring this form of comfort in my darkest nights. The pure joy that comes when I hear Him speak makes all the suffering worth it. In Paul's case, on that night, the words of Jesus carried him through the events of the next several years until he was taken home to Glory. He could draw strength and courage from those words as he appealed to Caesar, knowing this appeal could carry a death sentence.

The Voice of the Lord conveys with it this comfort for at least one other reason. According to that passage on comfort (I Corinthians 1), one of the reasons that the Lord allows His children to suffer is so that they will be able to pass His comfort on to others. Forgiveness and suffering are inseparably linked. If you want to know more about the process of forgiveness, consult the section on forgiveness, *More Blessed to Forgive* (p. 83).

Picture this: *since* the Lord can comfort you directly when you suffer in an area of your life, *then* you will be able to comfort someone else who is not able to be comforted directly by God with the comfort that He has given you. In this way, you will pass along His comfort to others. This is yet another way God can use to get people's attention and cause them to hear His Voice. He can use **you in your suffering to cause others to hear Him.** This could make the suffering worth it, if you are willing. By the way, if you are not willing, it is possible that you could be suffering without a cause, and this could be devastating.

5. Songs (Psalms)

One area in which I have many shortcomings is that of music. It is not that I cannot carry a tune or that my tone is annoying, but simply that I do not value music for the music itself. I'm not captivated by the beautiful voices, the harmonies, the instrumentals, or the rolling rhythm. I value music for how the lyrics move my heart.

The fact of the matter is that the Creator and Sustainer of the universe values it as one of His favorite methods for communicating with us. He even went so far as to dedicate a whole book in His Bible to this subject. Psalms is the longest book in the Bible and contains both the longest and shortest chapters in the Bible. The longest chapter (119) is about the Word of God, as well. All the Psalms were originally songs. Succinctly put, the most impactful Voice that the Lord utilizes is music.

When it comes to music, I often wax nostalgic. I remember the moments of pure joy as the Father reached into my inner core and triggered a connection with Him that moved me. I guess this was the purest form of heartfelt love. It was from these few encounters that I have been motivated to serve my Lord and Savior. His love compels me to action and songs triggered all of this.

5 Songs

The first was one night when I was about eight years old when our family went to see a concert in L.A. I think it was held at the Azusa Pacific College (now University) campus. My parents were good friends with Doug Oldham, who was the music guy at Skyline Wesleyan Church for a very brief time, I was told. We got special permission to sit on the front row. This concert was the first time that I remember being moved to tears at the presence of the Holy Spirit. The exact song was "God Gave the Song" and Gloria Gaither sang it. I was not captivated with her singing ability, although it was superb. I was moved by the Voice of the Lord that came through the song itself.

The song was about a tune that the Lord gave at creation. This tune was really the Lord Jesus Christ. It was a play on the John 1 preamble that declared that the Word was made flesh and lived among us. As the song progressed, the simple tune was tweaked and strained almost beyond recognition. This straining was due to sin. It was during this song that the Lord spoke to me. This was the first time that I can remember hearing from Him and knowing that He was speaking.

To my shame, I do not remember what He said. What I do remember was an overwhelming joy at hearing His Voice and recognizing it as such.

At this point, it is important to explain that I do not hear Him with my natural ears. Sometimes it feels like I can hear Him that clearly, but this was a spiritual hearing. Jesus was constantly saying something like, "He who has ears to hear, let him hear." I am starting to believe that this is the standard operating procedure for those who follow Christ. In fact, this is a very good definition for what a disciple of Jesus Christ looks like. **Disciples of Jesus Christ hear His voice and do what He says.**

Returning to my story, there I was, an eight-year-old, standing with my stomach touching the stage, looking up at Gloria Gaither (having no idea she was famous) while she sang a song that

Section 1 The Voice of the Lord

the Lord used to introduce His Voice to me. I wish I could say that there was a sudden aura of light that appeared around her head and the sound of angels tuning up their vocals, but there was none of that. Instead, it was a simple, ordinary song (I am quoting some of the lyrics), which the Lord interrupted in my heart as His matchless Voice broke through.

As I am writing this, even now, I have broken down in tears of joy. I am unable to explain why this memory is so very powerful, except that the Voice of the Lord is alive and powerful, able to cut like a scalpel, even to the joints and marrow, to determine the thoughts and intents of the heart. Maybe that Voice is even able to move an old person like me with the memory of it from a lifetime ago.

Since that day, the Lord has used songs in my life to remind me of two very encouraging facts. First, He reminds me that He is with me.

Second, He uses songs to let me know that I am on the right track. This track is only for me. I used to think that everyone should do the things that I was called to do. Then, when I was older, I realized that God was big enough to have an individual agenda for everyone. By the way, when we are listening, He is perfectly able to tell us what He wants us to do.

In the summer of 2000, I joined a team of medical missionaries on a relief mission to the war-torn villages of South Sudan. After the trip, we counted 13 very real opportunities for the whole team to lose our lives, not counting the individual opportunities. We arrived in one location as darkness fell over the landscape. By the way, when darkness falls in Africa, it is immediately and completely dark.

After we made our obligatory greetings, we asked for favor from the tribal leaders to be able to sleep among them for one night so that we could treat their sick the next day. After the customary hour of negotiation, they agreed to our request, and we set up our camp. This did not take long because we did not bring very much. This was our eighth day "in country" and our supplies were running low. It was then that we noticed the sound of sweet music in the distance. After asking our hosts for leave, we set off to investigate, following our interpreters.

It is important to understand that this was a refugee camp. About 20,000 people had run from the fighting that was nearby. They had stopped at this place with nothing but the clothing on their backs. They had only been at this place for two days when we arrived. Largely for the cause of Christ, they had lost everything to an army that was bent on their destruction. For security reasons, the only lights were small and intermittent.

As I stumbled along, struggling to keep pace with my Dinka guide, I began to hear the song get louder and more distinct. Whenever I would begin to make out one voice, many others would quickly swallow it up. It sounded like there was a leader, who would set a new pitch then an ocean of other harmonies would respond in pursuit. As I said, it was completely dark and lights were never lit to confirm what we witnessed. I have no idea how many hundreds of people were in attendance. I can only assume that these were black Africans and not an angelic host.

As we sat a few yards away, I began to count the harmonies that seemed to dance around the edges of the tune. Their descants were at the same instant, distinct and yet in resonance with each other. I stopped counting at 16 because at that moment, the main choir of thousands of voices launched into the chorus. All of this was in a dialect that was never fully identified, but my guide could make out the meaning of the chorus, after hearing it a few times… I weep as I recall the words:

> They attacked and took our land,
> They attacked and killed many,
> They attacked and burned our homes,
> They attacked and took our little ones,

Section 1 The Voice of the Lord

They attacked and stole our cows,
But the greatest thing, the greatest thing, the greatest thing, the greatest thing, is that **our sins** are forgiven.
They attacked and took our land,
They attacked and killed many,
They attacked and burned our homes,
They attacked and took our little ones,
They attacked and stole our cows,
But the greatest thing, the greatest thing, the greatest thing, the greatest thing, is that **their sins can be** forgiven.

Many in this choir probably did not live out that year. **However, they will join the choir that will surround the Throne on That day. We will sing with the syncopation of the rhythmic peoples and the accompanying expertise of the instrumental tribes; the families of soloists will finally blend and the maestros will guide the dynamics. On that day, all of us will have a part. Those of you who cannot carry a tune will sing, and your part will fit perfectly. We will all listen as your joyful noise accentuates the rest of us to showcase the Lord's marvelous grace.**

On that day, no one will be able to count the myriads of individuals lifting their voices in their various heart languages each understanding the others. **In unison, the song will crescendo as we turn to face the Lamb who was slain for us. A deafening silence will fall, as the counter-point to the song, while we instinctively fall on our faces before the Lamb.**

In my limited way, I have tried to punctuate the place that songs occupy as the Voice of the Lord. I know that I have not done it justice. Please take a few moments and ask the Father to remind you where He has met you in a song. Further, ask Him to meet you again on a deeper level. Remember that this Voice of the Lord is deep and powerful. On **that** day, we will all be glad that you rehearsed your part of the song.

6
Sleep

The Bible is replete with stories of how the saints of old have been warned and instructed through dreams and visions. Some of the most important decisions that have been made were influenced by dreams. From the visions of Abram and John to the dreams of the Josephs and Daniel, this was one of the more consistent ways that God accurately communicated to His servants.

The first time that dreams were utilized as a Voice of the Lord in the Bible was in the life of the patriarch, Joseph. (The story begins in Genesis 37.) This was certainly not the first time that dreams were thought of as a mode by which God, or the gods communicated to men. It was already an established fact that dreams were authoritative. Because they believed that dreams had deeper

Section 1 The Voice of the Lord

spiritual meaning, Joseph's brothers made a big fuss about the content of his dreams. Since then, dreams have been known as a legitimate Voice of the Lord. God routinely uses them to speak His mind to those who can hear Him in this manner.

I know a guy that takes afternoon naps in a tent in his spare room. He does this so that he can hear the Lord in his dreams. When he wakes up, he quickly writes down the details of his dream. He then goes and finds the person that he is supposed to contact. Very often this stranger gets healed and some find Christ. While his method of hearing the Lord's Voice may not always work, he is faithful to seek the Voice of the Lord in the mode that has been given to him.

Perhaps this is a Voice that the Lord can use to guide you. One word of caution is in order. This is a very subjective Voice. It absolutely must be in subjection to the other more objective Voices that we have already discussed—the most reliable of which is the Bible. Dreams are not meant to reinterpret or add anything to the Bible. The only acceptable use of this Voice is in practical application.

Another subset of this Voice is that of visions. Visions are like dreams in that both bring us to places that we do not visit in the awake world, and they cause us to experience things that do not historically happen. The difference is that visions are dreams that happen when people are awake. Biblically, God used both in the same manner and for the same result. Some people hold visions and dreams in high esteem, and the Lord can utilize these in their lives to move them powerfully.

The most notable of the Biblical visions is that of the Revelation of Jesus Christ, as penned by the apostle John. The Lord used this vision to present a detailed description of what was to come, as history was to unfold. Another well-known vision was presented to the prophet Daniel. He wrote some of it in the Biblical book that bears his name. However, the rest of what was given to

6 Sleep

Daniel was "sealed up," not to be revealed—at least not yet. Visions are the mode by which God communicated to several other prophets, as well.

We are not told how the Lord went about communicating with some of His servants. All too often, all we read is that the Lord told a prophet a message. One of these is important to our discussion. In the second chapter of Joel, God said that He was going to pour out His Spirit on all mankind. One of the blessings of this was to be the dreaming of dreams, and the seeing of visions. He was specific about the type of person who would receive these dreams and visions, as well.

In the second chapter of Acts, Peter quoted this prophecy and said that at least this part was beginning on that day. For this reason, I hold to the belief that you should have every expectation of hearing the Voice of the Lord in this manner. Remember, however, that the Cannon is closed. Any visions or dreams that you may have are given to you for you to apply the Bible to your life, not to introduce new theology or doctrine. Do not make the same mistake as Joseph Smith with his book of Mormon. Any message from the Lord will always totally agree and fully uphold God's previously revealed message, the Bible.

7
Seraphs or Servants (Angels)

Due to the understandable popularity of the Christmas message, the idea that God uses angels to communicate with us is well known. God used an angelic messenger, Gabriel, to give specific messages to vital individuals so that they would cooperate with His plan. For example, what would Mary have done when she found out she was pregnant, without being told how and why? Would Joseph have done his part without a clear message from God? It is safe to say that when God wants to motivate and direct us clearly, He often sends His servants, the messenger angels.

While it is safe to say that a very clear Voice of the Lord is these kinds of angels, it is also true that most angels are not messengers. Most angels may be classified as servants of the Lord, rather than communicators of His truth. In fact, I got a little happy with the "S" theme running through this book, so I fudged a little and entitled this chapter "Seraphs." The truth is that Seraphs are not messengers, ever. They are angels that live forever in the presence of the Father. Their full role and description may be found in the sixth chapter of the prophecy of Isaiah.

7 Seraphs or Servants

I, for one, really appreciate the role that angels have played in my life and ministry. One major role that many of them occupy is that of guardian. As I wrote earlier, I have had ample opportunities to move on to Glory during my service in the Kingdom. There are an unknown number of Guardians who have protected me thus far. In the book of Job, Satan referred to a hedge of protection that was defending the patriarch Job from the devil's attacks. I believe it was a band of Guardians. Since I have never lived in the spiritual realm, I cannot fully clarify where the line of God's personal protection begins and these guardian angels' protection ends. I do know that they are working under the Father's direction.

Despite our collective cultural understanding to the contrary, there are only a few messenger angels. They are not the highest or most powerful of the angelic host. They can be blocked from delivering their message. (See Daniel 10.) They can also visit us in visions and dreams. (See Daniel 8.) The subject of angels makes for a very interesting study. However, do not get carried away with this. Messages from true angels are clear and motivating, but they are also very rare, and they can be easily counterfeited. We do not get regular visits from angels, so we do not know what to expect. If we are looking for a visit from an angel, we might get a visit from the enemy who likes to dress like an angel of light (II Corinthians 11).

8
Self
(Theophany or Christophany)

All too often in the Bible, we are informed that a particular person got a word from the Lord and we are not told how it was transmitted. This can be frustrating for those of us who are trying to write a book on the Voice of the Lord. However, sometimes the Bible recorded that some individuals talked with the Lord face to face. This fact pinches correct theology in the nose because no human can see God and live. However, with a proper understanding of the role and nature of the second person of the Godhead (Christ) it is easy to see that this is possible. Jesus is God in a body. When people see God, they see Jesus.

The idea that God visits people is called a Theophany. As Trinitarians we would call this event a Christophany. In other words, Jesus visited specific human beings before He came as a baby in a manger. There are several clues that indicate this to the careful student of the Old Testament. Students of the Bible who were trying to distinguish a Christophany from an angelic appearance have discovered that sometimes a visitor who is called an angel does not act like an angel.

For example, sometimes a person who saw an angel said something like, "We have seen God" (Judges 13). Their conclusion was that they should be dead, because everyone knew that a person could not live once they saw God. The flaw in this kind of thinking was that Moses had conversed with God "Face to Face" regularly and he just glowed. This was a well-known, well-established fact.

8 Self

Another clue as to the true identity of an "angelic" visitor may be seen when the Biblical account refers to the angel as **the angel of the Lord** as opposed to **an** angel.

One of the most telling clues of the angelic encounter was whether the angel accepted worship. No self-respecting angel would ever allow himself to be worshipped. He would generally say that he was a fellow servant and raise the worshipper to his or her feet. However, when the person who was visited was actually in the presence of Christ, God would welcome the worship. I encourage you to do your own study of the Christophanies in the Old Testament. Yet, please accept two cautions on this Voice of the Lord.

Under no circumstances are we to ever look for or accept a visit from God, in Person. Jesus made this warning crystal clear. In Matthew 24, Jesus described some of the events and attitudes that would prevail in the last days. One of these would be the proliferation of false prophets and messiahs. Jesus warned that if someone says that a new messiah was in the wilderness or in an inner room, we should not believe it or act on the information. In contrast, He described how He really would come back to this earth. His return would be like lightning (fast) and like a thief in the night (secret). **For this reason, do not listen to any voice that says they (a visible person) are God or the Christ.**

The second caution is how the supposed messenger from God treats the Scripture (Voice #1). Messengers from God always uphold and rightly quote the Bible. They never get it wrong or reinterpret it. Their messages are brief. The idea that a messenger would come on multiple occasions and provide a complete book to someone like Joseph Smith is against all we know to be true about angels. They apply the Bible; they do not give renewed varieties of it.

Section 1 The Voice of the Lord

9
Situations or Circumstances

I have been deliberating for some time on the sequence of the last two chapters of this discussion. My original thought was to provide the Voices in order from objective and clear to subjective and fuzzier. Under this plan, this chapter would be dead last. However, the discussion has not panned out that way, and I have been rethinking the plan. The reason I am letting you in on this is because it is quite germane to the conversation. I have realized that believing that circumstances are a Voice of the Lord is a very normal belief. Despite this, circumstance is the most unreliable Voice there is if the other Voices are not present. **We simply cannot know what the Lord is saying based solely on circumstances.** We cannot even confidently know that He is directing us at all based on this Voice alone.

9 Situations or Circumstances

For example, Job's "counselors" were sure that Job's bad circumstances were indicating that the Lord was not happy with Job. This assumption was 180 degrees off the truth. The fact was that the Lord was proud of Job. He bragged on Job to the enemy. As those who are not living in the spiritual realm, **we have no idea what specific circumstances are supposed to tell us**, if anything at all. We must infuse the other Voices into the dialogue to understand what the Lord is saying with circumstances.

I am starting to believe that this Voice may occupy the role of punctuation concerning what God has to say to us. It is as though the Lord says, "such and such" with another of His Voices, and then He uses this Voice to add an exclamation mark "!". Perhaps the Lord may also use this Voice as an alarm to alert us that we are in danger or on a dangerous path. I am confident that when we get to Glory, we will have a good laugh at ourselves for all the weight and importance we gave this Voice when it stood alone.

10.
Still, Small Voice

On I Kings 19, the prophet Elijah had an encounter with God. This encounter was very important with respect to this Voice. As a matter of fact, it could be easily argued that this encounter is the core of this discussion. For this reason, I now request that you stop reading this book and go find a Bible. Read chapters 18 & 20 as well as the story of Elijah on the mountain of the Lord in chapter 19. Have you read it yet? Me too, again. Let us continue. For those of you who routinely preach or teach, there are at least 30 sermons in this passage.

The circumstances that led up to this encounter were significant. Elijah had heard the Lord before and their relationship was well established. In this encounter, there were terrifying circumstances. Elijah knew from previous experience that the Lord was not trying to tell him anything with these circumstances. The wind, earthquake, and fire were empty circumstances, provided to teach Elijah that God was in full control of circumstances and to

10 Still, Small Voice

teach us that circumstances may easily not mean a thing. Elijah knew that circumstances did not dictate anything to God, or His man. Elijah already knew, before the still small Voice spoke that he had messed up in coming to the mountain of the Lord. (We feel your proverbial pain, Elijah.) He did not need to come to the Lord for a "mountain top experience."

Elijah already knew the Lord's Voice. It was a very simple thing that the Lord wanted to teach him, and us. **All he needed to do was trust the Voice of the Lord and obey.** This is what true followers of Christ have always done. **This is what true disciples of Christ look like.** I do not understand all I know. This is simpler than that. The product of all our discipleship efforts needs to look like this. After a lifetime of intensive study on the subject, I can say that this is all there is.

I spent a few months in boot camp as a guest of the United States Navy. Our Company Commander (Drill Instructor) was nicknamed "Captain Pushup." You can imagine why he had this title. I and 49 of my best buddies learned to know his voice very well. Some of my fondest memories of him are the times that he would test both our knowledge of his voice and our immediate obedience.

There we were, out on the "grinder" marching in perfect 6x8 formation, when we would hear his voice from a hundred yards away, "A-Company-Halt." He had a very distinctive, singsong voice that struck the fear of pushups into our hearts. For this reason (push-ups), we failed to "halt" correctly only once. Every other time one step after this command reached our ears, we would stop in perfect unison. We knew that it was perfect because we would produce that sound with our feet that says, "perfection." All of us have heard this sound on television and in military movies. It is the sound that is made when the echo of marching feet suddenly stops.

After we had learned to immediately identify and obey the sound of his voice, Captain Push-up threw us yet another curve.

Section 1 The Voice of the Lord

He let his coworkers (other Company Commanders) try to stop us with their commands. Once again, the net result was more push-ups after we obeyed their other voices instead of only his voice. This taught us to only listen for one voice, distinguishing it from all others. Even though we were tested many times since that time, we never failed again.

When Jesus said that His sheep knew his voice (John 10), He also said that they (we) do not follow a stranger's voice. We need to be careful to listen only to the Voice of the Lord and reject competing voices. These may be other people, our inner voice, or even the enemy. We must do the work to be sure that we hear Him and do what He says, rejecting all others.

The very first and the very last thing that Jesus said to Peter was the same two-word phrase, "Follow me." (Compare John 21:22 and Matthew 4:19.) It is easy to follow Christ when He is walking the dusty trails, making footprints where He travels. However, following Him after He has ascended to the Father is another story. The interesting counterpoint to Peter's story is that he **did** exactly that. Inexplicably, he lived and moved about as his Master did with similarly fantastic results. One of the requirements of following Christ is to stop following others. Once a person can hear the Voice of the Lord, all other Voices must be muted.

Jesus stands at our door and knocks (Revelation 3:20). He will start with the ball-pin hammer of the still small Voice. If we fail to listen or even hear this poignant knock, He will upgrade. His next knocker will be the sledgehammer of a human's rebuke. This person could be a saint or a sinner. It does not matter who does the actual rebuking. If we fail to hear this abruptly intrusive knock, our Savior and Lord will upgrade His knocker yet again. His preferred tool for this last knock is a wrecking ball. It is not until we are picking through the wreckage of our scattered lives that some of us finally hear His Voice and follow Him.

10 Still, Small Voice

Conclusion

It is my hope that you begin to remember the times that the Lord has spoken to you in the past. Use this section to help you recall those special occasions where He has inserted Himself into your life.

If you have never done so, allow the Savior to introduce Himself to you. It is my firm belief that this is His highest goal for all of us, including you. I have written this section so that God will be able to use one of these Voices and someday say to you, "Hi, I am God. It is very nice to meet you. I really love you more than you know."

Section Two

More Blessed to Forgive

Dedicated to my one and only Savior, Jesus

Section 2 More Blessed to Forgive

Introduction

Evangelicals like to say that we do not promote religion, but rather a relationship with Jesus Christ. In truth, our faith is even more founded in relationships than this saying implies. All the major milestones of our faith are based on relationships. The two greatest commandments of Jesus reflect this.

When asked what the greatest commandment was, Jesus replied that love for God (with all our heart, soul, mind, and strength) and our neighbors (as ourselves) were the two commands upon which all the Law and the Prophets were founded (Matt 22:38-40). Jesus did not see fit to highlight the Ten Commands, or even the other 610 laws that God gave at Mount Sinai. Jesus emphasized love, both vertically with our Creator and horizontally with each other. Love is based in relationships.

The underpinning of all relationships is giving. Followers of Christ are giving people in general. The apostle Paul quoted Christ as saying that it was (and still is) more blessed to give than to receive (Acts 20:35). Paul recounted these words of Christ while giving his farewell address to a group of pastors. This was a very tearful time, and it could be argued that this message was one of Paul's most fervent sermons. His point was that he was a tent maker, so that he could give the Gospel to the people without asking them for money.

The extent (how much), duration (how long) and direction (giving, rather than taking) of giving defines relationships. I could say much on this subject. However, in this discussion, I have limited myself to a particular aspect of giving known as forgiveness. Because this type of giving happens in response to offenses, it may be rightly said that forgiveness is a gift of mercy and grace.

Introduction

Mercy is not giving someone the consequences that he or she may deserve for sinful actions. Christ provided mercy for the sins of humanity when He died on the Cross (Romans 11:32). As agents of the reconciliation process (causing people and God to be friends), we can extend this mercy to people. We love much because we were forgiven much. Part of showing this love to a lost and dying world is forgiving individuals for their offenses against us.

Jesus Christ gave both mercy and grace on the Cross for us. God really does love the world. He really did send Jesus to die on the Cross so that the world may be forgiven. He has called us to be His body. We are the picture of forgiveness for people who cannot see Jesus. We do this by being examples of forgiveness.

Christ has given the job of giving away grace and mercy to us. He has called us to be in the business of reconciliation. We are to extend God's gift of friendship to a lost and dying world through the message of the Gospel (II Corinthians 5:18-20). Christ died for our sins. Someone in my life passed the gift to me by telling me the message of the Gospel. I must pass this message on to those that do not know that Christ died for them. The problem is that people have trouble hearing our message.

It has been said that people do not care what you say until they know that you care. Re-gifting God's grace and mercy goes a long way toward showing people that we care for them. **Remember that mercy is not retaliating against people for their sinful actions. Grace is going one step further and giving them good things instead.** This is how God has treated us. We must pass this along to others.

One of the greatest gifts that we can give is forgiveness. The checkpoint here is that we need to forgive the way we

Section 2 More Blessed to Forgive

need to be forgiven. This is part of the Lord's Prayer. Praying this prayer is one of the few clear commands of Christ. He said when you pray, say, "Our Father which art in heaven... (Matthew 6:9-13 KJV). He provided a template or "go by" for us to follow when we pray. A good primer on this subject is written by Elmer Towns and is entitled *Praying the Lord's Prayer for Spiritual Breakthrough: Daily Praying the Lord's Prayer As A Pathway Into His Presence.*[4]

By the way, at the behest of one of my mentors, I did a comparative search in the Gospels on the way Jesus treated prayer in His life and ministry. I found that with respect to how Jesus seemed to view prayer, **sleep is optional, prayer is not.**

Since we need to be forgiven, we need to forgive first. After the Lord's Prayer, Jesus said that if we do not forgive, the Father will not forgive us (Matthew 6:15). The positive converse of this is also true (verse 14). When we forgive, the Father also forgives us. The prayer states, *"Forgive us our debts as we forgive our debtors"* (Matthew 6:12, KJV). Since this is what we are to say (in prayer), we would do well to forgive the way we need to be forgiven.

Do not let your theology keep you from following Christ's command. Many have been bogged down because they do not take Christ's words seriously. They argue that this is a "works theology" or some such nonsense, trying to explain away these "hard to swallow" words of Jesus. However, they would do well to remember that obeying Jesus is a huge part of what followers of Christ do. With respect to the charge that this is a "works theology," good works do not save us, however we have been saved *unto* (to do) *good works* (Eph. 2:8-10 KJV).

---

[4] Elmer Towns and Yonggi Cho, Bloomington, MN: Bethany House Publishers, 1997.

Introduction

Three Components to God's Forgiveness

There are *three components to forgiveness* that are at the heart of how God forgives.

First, He forgives **immediately** (rather than after we have suffered or learned our lesson). I do not know about you, but I want people who have hurt me to never do it again. I let them suffer for a while so that they will not forget how they hurt me.

God is far more gracious than me. He realizes that **time is the enemy when there is a need for forgiveness** and reconciliation (the renewal of friendship). God forgives **immediately**. There is a direct correlation between how much time has passed and how much work is required to repair a damaged friendship. The more time passes from offense to forgiveness, the more work will be required to repair the friendship (if it can be repaired at all).

Second, He forgives **completely.** This removes the **"*but*"** (i.e., I will forgive, *but* I **won't forget**). My excuse for not imitating God on this has been that I need to remember so that I will not trust the offender again. This will protect me from being hurt by that person again. There is an old saying, "Fool me once, shame on you; fool me twice, shame on me." Sadly, despite all this protection, the same individuals have still hurt me, repeatedly (usually people who are close to me).

God, on the other hand, **forgets** our sin. Psalm 103 tells us that our Heavenly Father has compassion on His children (us). He has promised to remove our sin as far as the east is from the west. That seems like a far distance to me. He forgives all our sin, and. He remembers them no more.

Third, God forgives without **condition.** This removes the "*if*" (i.e., I will forgive the offender **if** he does *blank*—*if* he stops hurting me or *if* he asks for forgiveness).

God's forgiveness is **unconditional.** He does not wait until we have cleaned up our act to earn His forgiveness. The

Section 2 More Blessed to Forgive

apostle Paul described, in Romans 5, the conditions of our forgiveness. We were forgiven before we had made any move toward righteousness. *While we were still sinners* (and sworn enemies of God), *Christ died for us* (Romans 5:8b).

Five Steps to Biblical Forgiveness

1. Identify the specific offense and describe the consequences in graphic detail (page 127). This is done best on paper. This may take time. It is important to enumerate all the details and possible ramifications. When true forgiveness is achieved, you will not want to need to forgive details that you overlooked in this step. Include the effect that the offense may have in the future on yourself and your relationships. This is especially important when the offense is against an intimate or protected part of your life. Secret sins seem to do the most damage over the long term.

2. Give the offense and the offender to Christ (page 129). Recognize that this offense has left a spiritual, social, physical, and mental deficit between you and the offender. He or she owes you a debt. This debt cannot be fully repaid by the offender. Even though it may feel like there could be satisfaction of this debt, there is no amount of vengeance that could undo the offense.

Begin the process by giving this debt to Jesus (in prayer). It was Jesus who paid the real cost (on the Cross) to redeem all sin debt. This step often takes a great deal of time and requires daily surrendering of sin debts to Jesus. Remember, He has forgiven you in the same way.

3. Find a way to truly thank God for (not in spite of) the offense, from your heart (page 131). This may take time, as well. Sometimes there is a change in you that has needed to come, in order to make your life's calling sure. There may be a shaping of your character that could only take place because of this specific offense. Never forget that the Lord Jesus said that fruit producers will be pruned by the Father as He cuts away parts of them, so that they will bear much fruit (John 15:2).

4. Begin to forgive during the offense (in cases where there seems to be no relief in sight) **(page 134)**. This does not mean that you need to stay in an abusive relationship when it is in your power to remove yourself. (See page 116.) We must, however, take care not to mislabel relationships as abusive and thereby give ourselves a reason for abandoning these relationships. Jesus modeled this step for us on the Cross. He stayed there (on the Cross) while He asked the Father to forgive them (the people who were killing Him). He later died due to their actions.

5. Change your story, from victim to victor (page 137). Christ is the victor, by the way. We must remember the words of the patriarch Joseph that they (his brothers) meant it (their violence against him) for evil, but God meant it for good.

Prolonged unforgiveness leads to bitterness. Bitterness leads to all kinds of physical abnormalities and diseases. Jesus' words on this subject have been confirmed by modern medicine. He said that it is not what goes into a man that defiles him, but rather what comes out, which is based on corruption within. It has been said that bitterness is the only poisonous pill that people take, hoping another person will die.

People who forgive like this will stand out in today's society. This is one of the best evangelistic tools at our disposal. However, many of us are so adept at overlooking and excusing offenses that we do not extend God's forgiveness, which is what people desperately need. We need to learn to be offended at sin, then forgive it. This will extend the forgiveness of Christ to a lost and dying world.

11

The Goal of Biblical Forgiveness

The idea that there is an objective standard for living is universal among human cultures. Some people see this idea as an uneducated, simplistic notion that is based on human superstitions. However, there are some measurable standards by which we all live. For example, we all feel that theft is wrong. My stuff is my stuff. If you take it from me, that is wrong. We all accept this and other standards to be true.

We have collectively and individually failed to meet these standards. When these standards are also decreed by God (in the

11 The Goal of Biblical Forgiveness

Bible), they are more than just mistakes when we fail to meet them. These failures are called sin. In the next few pages, we will explore what the Bible has to say about the subject of sin.

The study of Soteriology (or salvation) includes some subheadings like sin, human nature (before and after the fall), and the remedy that Christ provided on the Cross. However, this book section is not a theology treatise, *per se*. Rather, it is designed to cause us to feel that we can and should forgive. It is not enough to feel that we ought to forgive. Neither is it enough to feel guilty over not forgiving. The fact is that we must forgive in order to be forgiven by the Judge of the universe. In order to do this, we must first explore what the Bible has to say about forgiveness, since the author of the Bible is our Judge.

Eight Forgiveness Truths in the Model Prayer

Jesus' prayer life was so amazing that the disciples requested to learn to pray from Him. In chapter 11 of Luke's Gospel, they asked Him to teach them to pray. It is interesting that they asked Him to teach them *to pray* and not *how to pray*. The forerunner (John the Baptist) had taught his disciples *to pray,* and Jesus' disciples wanted something similar. John may have had some proper wording or guidelines that he passed along, and the disciples of Jesus wanted to hear if Jesus had anything similar.

Near the middle of the model prayer, Jesus mentioned the subject of forgiveness. Matthew also gave us a look at this prayer in his sixth chapter. In both Luke and Matthew's Gospels, Jesus used interesting words on this subject. Jesus did not simply tell His disciples to ask for forgiveness. Rather, He taught them to ask for the Father to forgive them as they were already forgiving others.

The remarkable wording of this part of the prayer tells us that we are to ask God to forgive us *in the future* just like we have

Section 2 More Blessed to Forgive

already forgiven *in the past*. If we can set aside our Calvinistic objections for a few moments, we may understand what Jesus was saying here. We may discover some nuggets concerning our need to forgive.

First, we need to **forgive prior** to asking for forgiveness. This seems to fly in the face of our understanding of faith. We rightly believe that nothing may be added to faith in the salvation process. This would include forgiving others as they do wrong to us. We do not need to forgive anyone in order to receive salvation and be forgiven by God for our sin. However, can we truly believe that forgiveness for our sins is possible while holding resentment (un-forgiveness for other people's sins) in our hearts? The tension at the heart of this question is real and deserves an answer. I am not sure I can adequately provide one. All I should say is that if you believe that this quandary might be applicable to your situation, err on the side of forgiving whatever might need to be forgiven.

I also believe that this idea is included at the end of the prayer that was given to the disciples as a model prayer. For this reason, I believe that the "forgive first" admonishment is reserved for those who are already forgiven for their sins and "In Christ." As always, I do not find apparent contradictions in the Bible as cause to disobey a clear directive. Since the Bible says to forgive, there is no viable reason not to forgive. We should be careful to forgive and let God sort out the theology of it.

Many of us have seen how resentment in a person's life has kept that person from hearing the truth of the Gospel. When we share the Gospel with someone they sometimes might say, "I do not want to join that bunch of hypocrites (in the church)." The story behind this protest is often that a churchgoer has offended this person, and the individual will not forgive the offense. The churchgoer's offense has caused the individual to not be able to come to Christ and be forgiven. The person must let go of the

11 The Goal of Biblical Forgiveness

offense, so that he or she may hear the Gospel and be forgiven by God.

Sometimes even followers of Christ have trouble forgiving. We need to keep in mind how low Christ had to stoop to forgive us. There is a tasty nugget to be found if we cross reference two passages on the *kenosis* or emptying of Christ. In the Philippians 2 passage, there is a description of the level and depth that Jesus reached to redeem (buy back from the slave market of sin) humankind. This passage is known as the *Kenosis* (emptying) passage.

Another passage, found in John 13 is a drama that Jesus played for His disciples on the night that He was betrayed. Both of these passages describe the steps that Christ took from glory to glory, winning our salvation. There will be a full development of these steps later in Chapter 12.

Second, the Father **forgives us the way we forgive others**. This idea should lead us to be more intentional and freer with our forgiveness. There should be no desire to punish or in any way delay our heartfelt, unrestricted forgiveness. Freely we have received, freely we are to give, or in this case, forgive.

Jesus told a parable to drive home the **importance** of forgiveness. In Matthew 18, He told the story of the king who wanted to settle accounts with his servants. One of these owed him an impossible sum, which he forgave. That forgiven servant went out and found the first person who owed him money, and demanded payment despite the pleadings of the borrower for mercy. When the servant began to take legal action against the borrower, some of the king's other servants told the king. The king took drastic action against the original servant who had owed him the great sum.

The obvious question is why did the servant who was originally forgiven do this? The answer is somewhat obscure. The ultimate reason was that he was not forgiven. In the king's mind, the debt was forgiven and in the past. In the mind of the servant, however, the debt was just beginning to be paid. He did not acknowledge that he had been forgiven the debt, so he began a mission to collect from those who owed him so that he could repay the debt. The point of this parable was that forgiven people need to extend this forgiveness to others.

Third, we need to **forgive the way we need to be forgiven**. For me this is especially difficult. I am a teacher by nature. I also do not want to waste anyone's time, least of all my own. For these reasons, I try to get the most mileage out of every circumstance (teachable moments). One of the most teachable moments is when there is conflict. I disguise my lack of forgiveness as a teachable moment. I try to make sure that the person who has crossed me will never do so again, ever. This, however, is not how I need to be forgiven. I must forgive rather than teach people lessons.

Fourth, we need to forgive **when** we are offended. This speaks to our need to be forgiven immediately. We do not need to be punished before God forgives us. This would certainly kill us for every offense. If God felt the need to teach us a lesson every time we needed to be forgiven, we would never get out of hell. If I want to be forgiven immediately, I must forgive immediately.

Fifth, we need to **forgive completely**. Most of us have heard something like, "I will forgive, *but* I will never forget." The need to be forgiven completely eliminates the "buts" from the forgiveness equation. What if God said something like this about us? Thankfully, He did not.

There is an Old Testament passage about how God treats us as His children. He removed our sins from His presence as far and the east is from the west (Psalm 103:12). Later, in the Prophets, He reinforced this by declaring that He remembers them (our sin) no more (Isaiah 43:25). Since these promises are applicable to us as children of God, we can *pay it forward* and forgive others completely.

11 The Goal of Biblical Forgiveness

Sixth, we need to **forgive without condition**. We experience a moment of power just prior to letting someone off the hook. This is because offenses of sin carry a spiritual debt. The offender becomes indebted to the victim. While this debt is quite intangible, it is real and felt by both parties in the sin equation. We will discuss this more later. As those who are offended, the victims are the ones to whom the debts are owed. When the "books" of accounting are opened on this sin, the person of power is the victim, much like the victim's statement phase in a criminal trial.

As those who are offended, we often devise conditions that must be met for us to grant our forgiveness. Rather than trying to conjure up conditions, we must learn to simply let go. Many of us have seen the last statement from the victim during this phase of the criminal trial go something like this:

"Although your crimes have hurt and deformed my life beyond measure, I forgive you."

I do not know about you, but I am moved to tears whenever I hear this. What the victim is saying is that vengeance for the crime is the correct action. However, the victim is choosing to let go.

One of my friends was rightfully convicted of crimes against a young woman. His two decades in prison led him to Christ. Decades after that, I heard him pleading with the Lord one morning for forgiveness concerning his crimes. He knew that the Lord had forgiven him. He was asking the Lord to cause that young woman to forgive him.

The **seventh truth is** that **forgiveness is not optional** for the follower of Christ. Further, the prayer that you should pray (the Lord's Prayer) pits you against yourself if you fail to forgive. **Lastly**, the way you forgive is the way you will be forgiven. So the **eighth truth** is to **forgive like your life depends on it**, because it does.

Section 2 More Blessed to Forgive

The First Sin

In the beginning God created us as morally positive beings. In this state, Adam and Eve were able to sin, but they had not fallen, yet. They soon erased this ideal situation by eating some fruit from the tree of the Knowledge of Good and Evil. This sent them and their offspring into a downward spiral of separation from their Maker. In His grace, however, God looked down through the ages with a plan to remedy this situation. He sent His beloved Son to be the price for buying them (us) out of slavery to sin.

Three Points of the Pure Gospel

In his book *Sin, The Savior and Salvation*, one of my mentors provided the clearest message of the Gospel I have ever seen. Dr. Robert Lightner argued that many of us blur the points of the Gospel, confusing our audience. He said that the pure Gospel contains only three points.[5]

The **first** task for the messenger of the Gospel is to review the subject of sin with the hearer. The goal is for the hearer to understand that all people have sinned. Continue this discussion by explaining that the wages of sin is death. This part should not be hurried through or skipped. In fact, the next part of the Gospel message should not even be broached until the hearer accepts that he or she is a sinner. This is the *question or problem* of the Gospel message.

The **second** part of the Gospel message, according to Lightner, is information concerning the person and work of Jesus Christ. The goal here is to provide the *answer* to the *question* of sin, the solution to the hearer's *problem*. There is no doubt that Jesus is the *answer* to life's most important *questions*. Jesus *answered* the *question* of sin by His death on a cross, two thousand years ago.

---

[5] Robert P. Lightner, *Sin, the Savior and Salvation: The Theology of Everlasting Life* (Nashville, TN: Thomas Nelson Publishers, 1991).

11 The Goal of Biblical Forgiveness

The **last (third)** part of the message of the Gospel, according to Lightner, is *personal acceptance*. The hearer needs to be able to say that he or she is a sinner, in violation of God's standard. He/she further needs to admit that he/she has nothing to expect from God, except judgment. Next he/she needs to accept that Christ died on the Cross for his/her sin. He/she needs to own the fact that Christ died for him/her individually and the whole world corporately. In essence, he/she needs to say, "That (the Gospel message) is for me." It is not enough that he/she belongs to some organization, or that his/her parents may be followers of Christ. There are no second-generation followers of Christ. Individuals must own the guilt and consequences of their own sin. They must freely admit that their sin was laid on Jesus.

The Debt of Sin

The understatement of the century is that I am a bad candidate for solving accounting issues. There are two reasons for this. First, I have real difficulty with multiple digits. When there are more than 5 or 6 numbers in a row, I tend to invert or switch the last two numbers. I especially have trouble with phone numbers. This is the lesser of the two reasons.

The real reason that I am such a poor accountant is because numbers bore me. One of the best ways to put me to sleep is to give me an arithmetic assignment. This is especially troublesome given the fact that I used to teach arithmetic to adults.

Section 2 More Blessed to Forgive

Having said all this about the riveting subject of accounting, I must admit that this subject has merit with respect to understanding forgiveness. In fact, I have no earthly idea how anyone is able to forgive any offense without some understanding of debt and accounting. There is no way to forgive someone without the idea that there is debt associated with offending someone. Many attempts have been made to forgive on a human level without this understanding. Most of these are coping mechanisms, rather than true forgiveness.

The Bible is loaded with passages on this matter. One of the more notable of these is the interchangeability between debt and trespasses in the Lord's Prayer. Jesus may have originally said a word that meant something like sins, or He may have said debts. Biblical scholars are still debating this question. However, it is entirely possible that He meant both. When a person harms another person, there is sin, and with it, there is debt.

Theologically, there is another whole category of passages that speak to this subject of sin-debt. When Jesus died on the Cross, He redeemed us back from slavery to sin. This slavery happened not because of a war, in which the victors carried off helpless victims as slaves. Rather, this kind of slavery is because of unpaid debt. Our sins have racked-up such a tab that we cannot pay the bill. We humans have sold ourselves into slavery to sin. There is no hope for us except the sacrifice of Jesus Christ. When He redeemed us (bought us back from sin) by His blood, He paid (the debt) for all sin and allowed us to live new lives.

When there is an offense, there is an entry placed in the debit column of an accounting book somewhere. The offender gives the victim an IOU slip with the offense. The offender does not always recognize this IOU marker. The offended person, however, is able to see it.

There is a balance of guilt and bitterness. One of the worst things a person can do is seek vengeance when dealing with being

11 The Goal of Biblical Forgiveness

offended. There is a very familiar passage in which the Lord forbade vengeance for good reason. He said that vengeance belongs to Him and He promised to repay (Deut. 32:35; Romans 12:19; Hebrews 10:30). The wording of this passage implies that there is a price associated with the offense. There is a debt that is incurred because of offenses. This debt cannot be fully satisfied by any human action. There is no amount of retribution that will suffice when justice (payment) is demanded.

When a person takes revenge on an offender, the person taking revenge inevitably realizes that vengeance is wrong. This realization is guilt. The offended person begins to weigh the act of vengeance against the bitterness that he feels over the original offense. This is the balance of guilt and bitterness. There will be more on this subject later in chapter 14. The process of forgiveness is the only escape from this trap.

The debt of sin is the idea that there is a marker that is passed to the victim at the time of the offense. As in all such markers, a third party may buy this debt. When a mortgage company buys a mortgage, the debt is no longer between the people who are buying the house and the original lender. The debt legally and in every other sense passes into the possession and ownership of the new mortgage company. This ability to transfer ownership of a debt is central to forgiveness in Christ.

Step two of the process of forgiveness focuses on this. This step is at the core of the forgiveness process. Only God can truly forgive sin. **Human beings cannot truly forgive anyone's sin. We are not in a place of judgment. We can forgive them the debt we feel they owe us, but that's all. That's why we must turn the offense and the offender over to Christ. Only He can offer eternal forgiveness and release them from eternal punishment.**

12
The Five Steps of the Kenosis (Emptying)

One day a man who was paralyzed was lowered into the presence of Jesus through a hole in the roof. Jesus was known as a healer. Everyone who was there probably thought He might do His bit and heal the guy. Unexpectedly, however, Jesus told the man that his sins were forgiven. This shocked His audience, so He healed the man as proof of who He was. The fact that Jesus was able to heal the man legitimized His pronouncement that the guy's sins were forgiven. His audience's objection that only God could forgive sin, was legitimate. Their assumption that Jesus was not God, however, was not legitimate.

Almost from the beginning of Christendom, the idea that Christ gave up a lot to save us has been a central message. In fact, the early church turned this message into a popular song. The song was probably called something like Kenosis (emptying). It is found in Philippians 2. The song went:

> Jesus Christ, who, being in the form of God,
> Thought it not robbery to be equal with God.
> But made Himself of no reputation,
> And took on the form of a servant,
> And was made in the likeness of men.
>
> And being found in fashion as a man,
> He humbled Himself,
> And became obedient unto death,
> Even the death of a cross.
> Wherefore God hath highly exalted Him,

12 The Five Steps of the Kenosis

And given Him a Name that is above every name:
That at the Name of Jesus every knee should bow,
Of things in heaven,
And things on earth,
And things under the earth:
And that every tongue should confess
    that Jesus Christ is Lord,
To the glory of God the Father.

This song was apparently a popular one. Paul used it as a reminder of the importance of a humble attitude.

In this song, we are able to see the five-fold movement of Christ in the salvation process. Step 5 reverses step 1, step 4 reverses step 2. Step three is the focal point of the acrostic:

Step 1: From Glory to Earth (implied)
  Step 2: From form of God to form of Man
    Step 3: Work of redemption (died on a cross)
  Step 4 From form of man to form of God (implied)
Step 5 From Earth to Glory

The **first step** in His movement was when He moved from glory to earth. This step was implied in the song. The fifth step involved the reversal of this step and was stated plainly. The movement in this first step took Jesus from the place of ultimate honor to the place of service. He did this willingly, at the behest of the Father.

The **second step** was for Jesus to shed His glorious appearance and don a servant's form. This was done as He was conceived and born of the woman, Mary. He no longer wrapped Himself in the light of the Shekinah glory as He had for eternity past. Showing His glory would have kept Him from accomplishing His mission of redeeming the world. He looked like any other man until it was time for Him to begin His active ministry. During His active ministry He healed the sick and injured. He did this as a testimony to His worth for the next phase of His ministry.

Section 2 More Blessed to Forgive

His **third step** in the process of salvation was going to the Cross. Jesus Christ paid for all sin on the Cross. He shed His own blood as a payment for our sin debt. The followers of Christ sang this in ancient times. They emphasized the deplorable nature of His death by reminding their hearers that it was not just death that He suffered, but death on a cross. Their contemporaries would have known that this was a public execution. In this step, Jesus did the work of redemption and paid for all sin.

The **fourth step** is also implied and is a reversal of the second step. The second person of the Godhead, Jesus, clothed Himself with His glory. He took up the Shekinah glory again and rewrapped Himself with light. This is a powerful image to think about because the glory of God burns away all that is unholy. We cannot imagine Christ in all of His glory and remain unchanged.

To put this into terms that we can grasp, let us remember John, the writer of the Revelation. In the first chapter, he wrote a description of the fully glorified Christ. He included his reaction to Christ in this form. In the seventeenth verse John said that he fell at Christ's feet as a dead man.

Think of it, the beloved (by Jesus) disciple meets the fully glorified Christ and falls down as a dead man. The sight of the Shekinah glory of Christ decimated the disciple, John. This was the disciple who had comfortably laid his head on Jesus' chest during meals. The fact that John was very comfortable in Jesus' presence during His earthly ministry did not prepare him for the image of the ascended Christ. We cannot imagine the power of the presence of Jesus in His true form.

The **fifth and last step** was the movement from the place of service to the place of honor. The Lord Jesus Christ again sat down at the right hand of God the Father and regained His place of ultimate honor. This was His rightful place in the universe. He will forever be glorified as He occupies this seat of power and glory. He will forever occupy this seat, even when He is scheduled to be

12 The Five Steps of the Kenosis

elsewhere doing other great works. This is only part of the picture of what it means to be the second person of the Godhead.

The Same Five Steps Demonstrated

There is a narrative that the apostle John recorded in his Gospel that is a magnificent picture of these steps and movements in the redemption story. In the thirteenth chapter, John documented the washing of the disciples' feet. He is the only one to tell this story. It fits the theme of his Gospel perfectly. Many have debated whether followers of Christ should actually wash one another's feet. Some denominations have divided over it. However, for this discussion, let us simply read the story.

It was the night that the Passover meal was to be eaten. Jesus knew who He was, where He had come from and where He was going. His love for His own was an everlasting love that would last to the end. The grand evening meal was being served. At this meal Jesus got up from the table. This was a very unusual thing for Him to do.

I do not know what place Jesus occupied at that table. However, we know that He would've been in the seat of honor. The eaters reclined and John was using Jesus as a pillow. Jesus reclined at the proverbial head of that table. It was from this place of honor that He moved to the place of service, which is the **first step**.

I was raised in a household where there were strict rules. One of the strictest parts of our day was dinnertime. My father had many convictions that were quirky and cute to outsiders. One of these was his belief that he should not get up from the dinner table. He had a signal that he employed to this end when he wanted to have more tea in his glass. He called it the ancient Chinese tea ceremony. He would pick up his glass and rattle the ice that was in it. This would signal to one of my sisters that they needed to get up from the table and get tea to pour into his glass. One of them would get up and fill his glass and thus move from the table to the place of servanthood.

What my father was trying to teach us was that the person at the head of the dinner table was the person of honor and was not to get up from the table. If my father did get up from the table, and it was not for personal hygiene purposes, this would be a break from protocol and would place him in the role of a servant.

When Jesus got up from the meal on that night, **He was moving from the place of honor to the place of servanthood**. (By the way, the ancient Chinese tea ceremony died with my dad.)

This is precisely what the second person of the Godhead did when he came to earth as a human being. He moved from the place of ultimate honor and glory to a place of servanthood. This was the first step in His redemptive work on humankind's behalf. This step was so enormous that it is impossible for us to even imagine, much less quantify it on paper. Think of it, the perfect, holy king of the universe came to *this* place.

When my sisters got up from the dinner table, they moved from their rightful place at the table, to the place of servanthood as tea servers. They did not, however, change their appearance to look like servants. I suppose they could have put on an apron or something, however, they never did. When they were reseated to continue their meal, they took up their rightful position at the table.

Jesus did much more than this when He left His throne in Glory. He did not come as the grand king that He was, but as a lowly baby. **This is condescension to an unreasonable digression.** He was *that* high and we are *that* low.

After Jesus made His **first move** by **getting up from the dinner table**, He **took off His robe and wrapped a towel around His waist.**

In that time there were no photographs. Paintings of important people were rare, and they usually were hung in places where most people were forbidden to go. For this reason, what a person wore was designed to signify their place or station in life.

12 The Five Steps of the Kenosis

The color and complexity of their clothes often told the people with whom they were interacting that they were someone of prominence. Royal blue and purple were colors that were often reserved for people of a royal position and not for commoners. The Jewish people of Jesus' day expected their leaders to wear garments that signified that they were leaders.

It is apparent that Jesus wore this kind of outer robe from two encounters in His life. People who could not know Jesus as a Rabbi or teacher addressed Him as such. This could have been because someone who *did* know Him pointed him out, or it could have been His outer garment that gave Him away. On the Cross His executioners did not want to rip His robe into pieces, so they cast lots for it. This was because it was a fine robe. This robe showed those around Him that Jesus was a significant person. Jesus took this robe off in order to put on the garb of a servant

When I was a kid, I liked to watch Bible movies. These were classics like *The Ten Commandments*, or *Ben Hur*. The reason I liked these was because they were the only ones I could watch (my father was strict about this), and I was a movie buff. One thing I noticed quickly was that I could identify who the boss was by what he was wearing. He would wear the best, most colorful robes. Conversely, I could also tell who the slave was by his dress. Servants and slaves did not wear much at all. The women would don a simple rough dress and the men would work in nothing more than a towel that was wrapped around their waists.

What Jesus did in this **second step** was to **take off His glory and don the human form of a servant**. This is, again,

Section 2 More Blessed to Forgive

unimaginable. His light-filled Shekinah glory was removed, and He moved into the form of a helpless baby. He was subjected to the need to be washed and to have his soiled diapers changed. He was subjected to the will and whim of anyone bigger. After being the most immense being in the universe He became small. In the universe that He had created and sustained for several millennia, He became one of the puniest of inhabitants. This was such an incredible condescension that I am at a loss for words to describe it. I am in tears of gratitude while I am trying to write this. Pray with me.

We praise you, Lord Jesus; because you have not left us in the lowly place that our sins stationed us. Instead, you visited us in our low estate and forgave the guilt of our sin. You condescended so far that we cannot comprehend the plunge. You did this at the behest of the Father.

We praise you, Heavenly Father; because you sent your only Son to be abused by us in such a manner, that you could lay on Him all sin. This defies all understanding and is the epitome of love.

Amen

I am so very glad that He did these first two steps for us. Without His coming to this world as a lowly baby, Jesus would not have been in a position to finish His work on our behalf. An interesting study may be found in tracing the times and circumstances that Jesus hid His true identity. He did this as a continuation of this second step. If His glory had been revealed before He was nailed to the Cross, would the angry crowd have cried out, "Crucify!?" I think not.

While these first two steps are unimaginable, the **third step** goes far beyond, into the land of the impossible. The third detail that John recorded for us was that Jesus began to **wash the disciple's dirty feet, drying them with the towel that was wrapped around Him**. This act has been studied and imitated for the past two thousand years. It has been memorialized in countless ways. It was acutely brought to my attention several decades ago by a

12 The Five Steps of the Kenosis

bronze statue that was placed in one of the courtyards at Dallas Theological Seminary.

This statue showed someone posed as Jesus washing the foot of someone posed as one of the twelve disciples. Some of the other students and I began to spend our lunchtime at this statue. We would sit in silence and ask the Lord to teach us while we ate. In the year that followed, I learned some seemingly trivial details. One of these was that 24 feet got washed that night. However, there were 26 feet in the room. Another detail was that Jesus had to look where He was working. It is interesting that the two feet that did not get washed were attached to Jesus. This was on purpose. He alluded to the fact that this foot washing was more meaningful than regular foot washings.

Regular foot washings were concerned with the cleanliness and comfort of the foot being washed. The goal of the foot washer was to cause the indoor spaces to not smell like the outdoor spaces. The reason this was necessary in Jesus' culture was because the people did not wear shoes. At best, they wore sandals. Adding to the dirt that collects on unshod feet was the fact that they did not have vehicles in which to ride. The way most people moved from one place to another was on foot. Adding yet more to the dirt that collects on unshod feet was the fact that the roads were almost all unpaved. This meant that dust was on every road. The amount of dust was compounded by the fact that the region that Jesus lived in was arid without much rainfall. The lack of abundant vegetation led to even *more* dust.

All of this dictated that upstanding households would employ someone to wash their guest's feet. It was customary for a supper such as this one to be preceded by foot washing. If there was no such servant in the household, the person of lowest station was expected to perform the deed. There must have been some awkwardness during this time as to which disciple was the lowest, the understood designee for this task. The tension must have been

Section 2 More Blessed to Forgive

building. Perhaps the disciples felt that this custom was going to be ignored. Then the Lord stood up and took off His robe.

John unemotionally recorded that Jesus wrapped a towel around His waist. However, this act probably made the disciples very uncomfortable. They must have realized that He was about to break all customs and protocols. The master was going to wash the servants' feet. This could not be so.

This was the objection that Peter leveled at Jesus when his turn came. Much has been made of the comedic interaction that followed. Peter pronounced that Jesus would never wash his feet. In the next breath, Peter asked Jesus to give him a bath.

As a side note, breaks with protocol are how the Master often works with us.

There is a hint during this interaction that Jesus was doing more than foot washing. Jesus said to Peter that unless He washed him, Peter would have no place with Christ. A normal foot washing would not carry this kind of weight. This foot washing carried more meaning. However, when uncovering what Jesus meant by this, we must be very careful not to violate a crucial interpretive principle.

One of the non-negotiable principles of hermeneutics (a big word for interpretation) is that there is one meaning to each passage of scripture. Further, the plain meaning is the best meaning. In some theological circles, there is a tendency to look for a hidden, more spiritual meaning beneath the obvious one. There can sometimes be no end to the abuse that the Bible endures for someone's theological agenda.

For example, when one of the Gospel writers included the number of fish that the disciples caught when throwing their nets on the other side of the boat, some groups like to theorize a hidden message. However, the truth is that this number is just a number meant to communicate that there were a lot of fish. There is no hidden agenda or message in the exact number. Please do not look for hidden messages in the Bible. **The rule is that when the plain**

12 The Five Steps of the Kenosis

sense makes perfect sense, look for no other sense because this would be non-sense. The only exception to this rule is when the Bible says there is a hidden message.

When Jesus washed the disciples' feet, He gave us just such a clue. In John 13:7 Jesus said that Peter did not understand what He was doing, but later Peter would understand. If this were a normal foot washing, Peter would have understood it very well. However, Jesus had a deeper meaning than simple foot washing.

Jesus was providing a drama or memorable action that would demonstrate His entire work on their behalf. He knew that He was going to the Cross in a few hours. He wanted the disciples to know the full scope of His love. This is precisely the alternate reading of John 13:1. He showed them His love, all of it, in a play that included all five movements that are found in the song of the Kenosis (Philippians 2).

The Climax of it All

The climax of this tragic yet glorious story was step 3. In this word picture narrative, Jesus washed the disciples' feet with water and a basin and dried them with the towel that was wrapped around Him. The historical event that the foot washing signified was the work of redemption (buying us from sin). This included His death, burial, and resurrection. The full scope of what it took for Jesus to endure this is incredible. If it has been a while since you read the details of what killed Jesus, it might be a good idea to re-read it on pages 53-57 of Section One.

The Kenosis in Philippians 2 was a brief recapping of this emptying that Jesus endured on our behalf. The third movement of

Section 2 More Blessed to Forgive

Jesus in that upper-room portrayed this for the disciples. He washed the dirt off their feet, using only water and a towel.

When I was a boy, I did not like to wash with soap. I would rinse my dirty body off in the shower and then dry with a towel. I could not fathom how my mother knew that I did not use soap. Then one day I looked at the towel after I had dried. It was filthy. My mother only had to inspect the towel to see that I had not used soap.

If we were able to go back and inspect the towel that was wrapped around Jesus' waist, we would have seen a very dirty towel. The dirt that 24 feet had on them would have definitely stained the towel that was wrapped around His waist. John then recorded that Jesus **put His majestic robes back on and sat down**. Paul recorded **these last two movements** in Philippians, saying that Jesus was exalted. Both renditions record that Jesus finished His work by replacing His Shekinah glory and taking His rightful place, seated at the right hand of the Father. The obvious question is, what happened to the towel?

In another book that the apostle John wrote (Revelation), Jesus was constantly described as the Lamb *Who was slain*. Christ was still carrying the marks that took our sins away. This is why the risen Jesus could show Thomas and the other disciples His wounds. I do not know how far into eternity He will carry these marks, but I do know that it will last until the end of time.

As I write these words, I am full of awesome thanksgiving once again at the extent of Jesus' love for me. It is no wonder that John began this narrative with the encapsulating phrase, "He (Christ) now *showed them the full* extent of His love (John 13:1b)."

13

Human Alternatives to Forgiveness

While there are many good reasons for us to forgive each other, we are a rebellious race. We would often rather have our own way, even if it kills us. Forgiveness is not a normal part of our fallen nature. Many of us are like the trapped monkey who will not let go of the free food in the gourd. The trapper is able to walk up and capture him because the monkey is too greedy to let go and run to freedom.

Let's look at some of the more common alternatives (excuses) to true forgiveness. Now the purpose of this list is not so you can see your favorite excuse and feel comforted that you are "normal" and continue choosing to not forgive. No! If the Holy Spirit convicts you, do not hesitate to repent from things on this list. None of us are immune from the disobedience of not forgiving.

Section 2 More Blessed to Forgive

Overlooking the Offense, not really

This one is a little bit misunderstood. Proverbs says that it is to a person's glory to overlook an offense. It reasonably follows, then, that as cohorts of Christ we should routinely overlook offenses in order to obey this directive. However, the reality of the situation is that we do not overlook the offense. We simply do not confront the offender. We call this overlooking the offense. There is a delicate balance here that needs to be understood. If we are honestly able to know that the offense means nothing to us, we have overlooked the offense. If we rehearse the story to others (gossip), we need to begin the process of forgiveness.

Brooding

It seems that everyone has his or her pet sin. This is one of my many pets. One of my first responses to an unjust situation is to shut down all communication. My lovely wife refers to it as pouting. This label usually goads me to anger, which leads me to realize that I need to start the forgiveness process. Not that I always do, but at least I know that I have a problem.

When someone is brooding, they find it difficult to think about anything but the offense. They rehearse it in their minds until deep-seated resentment develops. This resentment can easily develop into hatred and, if left unchecked, death. Remember, anger and hatred are like murder (Matt 5:21-22; I John 3:15-17) When God confronted Cain about his brooding, Cain was already at this level concerning his brother, Abel. God said that sin was crouching at Cain's door, waiting to devour him. Cain needed to radically alter his thoughts in order to avoid murder. Sadly, he did not. Will I? Will you?

Ignoring the Offense and/or the Offender

The idea behind this one is that if we ignore the problem or the person, they will just go away. The reality is that problems, left alone, tend to get worse, not better. Professional athletes

13 Human Alternatives to Forgiveness

sometimes like to try to ignore the pain of an injury and keep playing. However, races that are run on broken ankles tend to be short. The pain is simply too great to continue. We need to face problems and people with the same grace and mercy that was extended to us by our loving heavenly Father. We need to forgive.

Going to Your Happy Place

One of the reasons I began the process of discovering true forgiveness was a book that my mother gave me. It was a book on forgiveness. It was based on a study that was conducted by a secular group concerning the need for and the steps of forgiveness. The problem was that they completely left Christ out of the process. I am of the conviction that true forgiveness is impossible without the work that Jesus did on the Cross. There were nine steps in the book's process. The first step and the last step were somewhat like those I have proposed in this book. However, this was where the similarities ended.

They used the middle seven steps to essentially encourage their readers to go to their happy place. Their participants were provided with coping mechanisms in an apparent effort to encourage them to forget the offense. Unless strong pharmaceuticals are employed, this is impossible in cases where the offense is significant. Even *if* the offense could be forgotten, forgetting is not forgiving. These are two entirely different outcomes. There simply is no forgiveness without Christ.

I would be remiss in both my education and experience as a mental health amateur provider if I did not insert more concerning the use of the "Happy Place." This term is widely used in some sectors as a flippant term meaning someone's place that they go in their minds in order to avoid unpleasant realities. Neither the authors of the above-mentioned books on forgiveness nor I are using this term in this way. What is meant by this term is a pre-established safe memory (whether real or imagined) into which a

Section 2 More Blessed to Forgive

therapist can take a mental patient when therapies become too intense. It is also an effective tool for coping with general negative emotions that a person may encounter in non-therapeutic environments. What I am saying is that this is not forgiveness. It is a temporary quick-fix that does not last.

Talking About the Offense with Others

While this tactic may seem to be beneficial at the beginning, it is simply gossip and sin. I know that it feels good to be affirmed by a third party, but it is wrong for me to include someone else in my interpersonal conflicts. There is One who is ready, willing and able to hear about the trouble that another person has caused. He has already forgiven them. He wants you to do the same. If it takes confrontation in order to accomplish this, so be it. Go to the offender—privately—if it's safe to do so—and fix it.

Excusing the Offense for Whatever Reason

There is a tendency among parents of young children to do this. As I am writing this, I am on a flight sitting beside a grandmother. Her five-year-old grandson is sitting beside her and acting up slightly. It is easy to see what is on her mind. She is probably excusing his behavior because of his young age. This is normal because children tend to act like children and grandmothers tend to think like grandmothers. However, when 21-year-olds act like toddlers, it is no longer normal or understandable.

We need to begin to stop excusing bad behavior. If we are offended, our first response should be to forgive rather than to excuse. If we say some offensive behavior is "Ok" because of some arbitrary reason, then we are excusing rather than forgiving.

There is another mindset behind excusing rather than forgiving. If we say that someone is forgiven when they ask for it, we may feel like we are acting superior to them. They may resent our words of forgiveness as some kind of high-handed gesture.

13 Human Alternatives to Forgiveness

The real issue, however, behind not wanting to utter the words, "I forgive you," is our true understanding that we are giving up our only recourse. We are giving away our right to compensation. This feels like a loss. The second step of forgiveness speaks more on this subject (p. 88). At this point it is sufficient to say that the person who forgives from the heart experiences a loss. Do not shy away from this loss. Jesus will meet you there and be enough.

Belittling the Offender

This can be done with words to others or may be done in our mind. We are repeatedly warned in the New Testament, however, that judging another person is out of bounds. We may be attempting to excuse their behavior, or we may be trying to find comfort in the conversation with a third person, but it is still wrong. We need to find our comfort from the Father, in prayer.

On this subject, it is a good idea to become very familiar with the book of Psalms. Some of the chapters are songs that have grown out of prayers. Many of these prayers are called imprecatory prayers. These are called this because the person who wrote them was very angry with someone. The wording of some of these is graphic and powerful. The Psalmist pours out his venom to the Lord. This is a godly way to pray when someone has hurt you.

When you engage in this kind of prayer, be ready for two things.

First, be ready for God to comfort you and cause you an inexplicable peace.

Second, expect God to change your heart toward that person. After all, He *did* die for *that* person, as well.

Disparaging Yourself because of the Offense, as if You Deserved the Offense

I have more to say on the subject of forgiving yourself in Chapter 17. However, the mindset behind this does not always stem from the perfectionism that I describe in that chapter.

Section 2 More Blessed to Forgive

Sometimes an offended person honestly feels that they deserve an abusive situation. If this is you, I implore you to get help. This is a very dangerous mindset. I believe the evil one is using it to destroy you and your children. I will speak more on the subject of abuse below, but please listen to me now. GET OUT! RUN AWAY!

When We Need to Sound Spiritual, We Say We Will Pray About It

When something is brought to my attention that requires action, it is my duty to act. This includes reconciliation (repairing friendships after an offense). I do not need to ask God what I should do when He has already given direction in His Word. At this point, inactivity is sin. What I really need to pray for is boldness as I find the person that I have offended (to be reconciled). The same is true when I need to let them know that I have forgiven them.

We Label the Offense Abuse

I broach this subject with great fear and trepidation. There needs to be clarity of thought here on a level that few of us reach. Misunderstandings in this arena may lead to trauma and perhaps even violence. I do not want to give the impression that a person in a truly abusive relationship should somehow tough it out and stay in that situation. If there is any doubt, please reread the paragraph at the top of this page. Please consistently err on the side of safety and security for yourself and your children. However, there needs to be a balance between mislabeling a situation as abuse and the real deal.

If a person is in an apparently abusive relationship, care must be given to establish the facts of the case before any labels are applied. Flippantly calling a person an abuser is libelous and immature. Mislabeling a person as an abuser can lead to as much trauma

13 Human Alternatives to Forgiveness

as keeping a victim in a truly abusive relationship. By the way, anger is not abuse. It often leads to forms of abuse, but by itself, it is not abuse.

There are some clues to help in an assessment of a potentially abusive relationship. The *first* of these I have referred to previously. If the victim feels that she is somehow deserving of abusive behavior, something is wrong. Proverbial red flags should go up in the assessor's mind. This person and her children need to be removed from the situation. The authorities may need to be included in this process. There is a real danger here. This situation is not to be taken lightly.

The *second* clue concerns current proximity. There are several questions that need to be asked and answered. Are they still in the alleged abusive relationship? Was there a running battle between the two of them? What do live-in adult witnesses say about it? How long ago did the situation end? Were the police ever called? Is the tone sorrowful or angry? If these questions are not enough to convince you not to label abuse quickly, check your own motivations.

All I am saying here is that there is a trend among *amateur* family counselors (they used to be called gossips) to arbitrarily label some situations as abusive. The supposed victim then takes this label and beats the supposed abuser over the head with it. This practice is wrong. It is used to violate the most concrete commands concerning the need for forgiveness.

14

The Balance of Guilt and Bitterness

A generation ago my father created a ministry around his marriage and family counseling practice. He had much to say about the subject of forgiveness. I have many humorous quotes tucked away on the subject. One of his favorite talks was on the topic of the growth of the Lord Jesus Christ from the time He was 12 until He began His earthly ministry. His text was chapter 2 of Dr. Luke's Gospel, verse 52.

After restating four aspects of Christ's growth (Jesus grew physically, intellectually, spiritually, and socially), my father would launch into a compelling and humorous look at the balance of guilt and bitterness. What follows here is a feeble attempt at an imitation of this insightful talk. To my knowledge, it has never been reproduced elsewhere.

14 The Balance of Guilt and Bitterness

"Jesus grew socially. This usually means that a person grows in their interpersonal skills. They know when to speak and when to be silent. They learn when to mourn and when to laugh. They learn how to generally relate to people. One of the more important lessons that a person must learn is how to handle interpersonal conflict. For this reason, I need to ask you a few questions so that we may gauge your development in the area of social growth. The first one is, 'Who do you hate?' In response to the stunned looks on the audience's faces he would ask, 'Why do we look so shocked?'

"When I ask who do you hate, I know that we are all good people here, and we do not hate anybody because that would be sin. So I will ask the question another way, 'Who do you wish would just go away?' 'Who, when they come in that door, makes you want to beat a hasty retreat out the other door?' You had a name pop into your head just now didn't you? If you have a name, you have a problem. So, whom do you hate?

"You know why you hate that person? It is because of unresolved conflict. They have done something against you and you refuse to forgive them. This has continued long enough that a root of bitterness has grown up inside you and is defiling you and your family. You have a real hard time with what she has done to you.

"To complicate matters, you have exacted some form of revenge. You have retaliated. You have done something to get even with her and you feel some twinge of guilt over it. You did not feel much guilt, at first, but over time the guilt has become unbearable.

"You know that you should not have done it, but you thought that you would feel good if you did it, to get even with what she did to you. It is hard to sleep at night, remembering what you did out of vengeance. You did not hide the fact that it was you who did it and that you did it to get back at her. It didn't feel as good as you thought it would though. The look of betrayal that she gave you when she realized how you had hurt her is still haunting you.

Section 2 More Blessed to Forgive

"There is this struggle in your heart. On the one hand, you feel guilty for what you did to her. On the other hand, you cover the pain of your guilt by rehearsing what she did to you. The more you rehearse these two hands, the heavier they seem to become. Both of your hands seem to be so weighed down that you cannot do or think about anything else. It is as though you have spent every waking moment, for as long as you can remember, balancing your guilt with the bitterness. The more you think about it, the heavier it gets. It is as though you are about to…collapse."

At this point my father would pause and slowly look around the room. He had been miming the whole process that he was describing by allowing his two hands to get lower and lower the more he talked about the balance of bitterness on his left hand and guilt in his right hand.

He was showing how heavy they were becoming, and the audience was feeling it. This pause was almost unbearable to most of the people that heard him give this talk. His face would get redder and puffier as he would struggle to bear the load on his hands.

When it seemed that all he could do was collapse under this load of guilt and bitterness, he would begin to talk again. He would say, "Wouldn't it be nice if there were some place to put all of this guilt and bitterness? Wouldn't it be great if there were someone, that we could give all this garbage to, so that He could carry it for us?"

He would pause before declaring, "There is."

He would then raise his hands to form a cross. He would say, "Give it all to Jesus." *Casting all your cares upon Him, for He cares for you* (1 Peter 5:7 NKJV).

14 The Balance of Guilt and Bitterness

As the early Christian apologist in 200 AD, Tertullian says:

It is only when we give all sin to the Lord that we find relief. He not only paid for and forgave my sin, but also yours. He does not want me to experience forgiveness, without extending it to those who offend me. I will be able to feel no forgiveness, until I pass it on to those who harm me. This forgiveness must extend to those who wrongfully persecute me for righteousness sake. When they shed our blood and we do not retaliate, the whole world takes notice. We must not forget that it is the blood of the martyrs that is the seed of the church [6]

There are two passages in the first Gospel that directly deal with this issue from two different perspectives. The first one is Matthew 18. In this passage, Jesus addressed the issue of how to deal with a brother who offends you. Jesus said that when your brother offends you, go to him privately and confront him about his sin. If he repents, you have regained your brother. If he does not, you need to make a second trip and take some witnesses. If he still does not listen, you need to take him before the church. If he rejects the ruling of the church, you are to not associate with him. At every turn, the goal is repentance and reconciliation. If he repents at any time, the correct response is forgiveness. In case there is any confusion on this passage, let me make it clear. When your brother sins, go to him for repentance and reconciliation.

This passage deals directly with my dad's first question concerning who we may hate. We must learn to go directly to those who have wronged us and fix the relationship. Remember, time is the enemy of this process. Also remember that third parties muddy the waters. The more time you allow to pass, the more time the enemy will be able to ensnare you in division and deceit. The more people who know about the offense, the more people will weigh in with their divisive advice and opinions. I need to heed this warning myself on a daily basis. None of us are immune from being the enemy's mouthpiece on this subject.

---

[6] Tertullian, Quintus Septimus Florens Apologeticus, L. 13, translation by Alex. Souter with introduction by John E B Mayor, Cambridge University Press, 1917.

Section 2 More Blessed to Forgive

The second question my dad would ask was who hates you? When my dad would ask this question, he would often get a similar response to the first question. Many in the audience would start fidgeting in their seats. He would quickly rephrase the question into a more palatable one.

"Who does not like you? Who wishes you would just go away?"

If you have a name, you have a problem. The second passage on this subject is found in Matthew 5:23-24. In these verses, Jesus placed gaining reconciliation above giving an offering in terms of primacy.

In this passage, Jesus said that if you are giving an offering and there remember that your brother has something against you, leave the offering and go to your brother. After he has forgiven you, then come back and give the offering. This is remarkable, given the high priority some of us put on offerings. Maybe our priorities need some adjustment."

At this point, my dad would begin to offer some practical advice on how to reconcile with a person who has something against you. He would visit the subject of restitution. This is the idea that there are consequences that follow our sin. These consequences sometimes carry a heavy price tag. *God* may have forgiven our sin, but *our neighbor* wants cash. When we have sinned, we need to be ready to pay. I know this flies in the face of how we are treated by our loving Heavenly Father. However, this is the way of men.

After he gave this talk, my father was always inundated by questions from those individuals who were sure that their case was the exception. They had convinced themselves that their sin against someone else was too great to ever be forgiven, or that the sin against them was so grievous that it was in a special class. In response, he would remind them that Jesus paid for all sin.

By the way, the follower of Christ's responsibility in both cases is the same. We must go to our brother and reconcile. If our brother ever comes to us and seeks reconciliation, we should feel embarrassed

14 The Balance of Guilt and Bitterness

that we did not go to him first. We should quickly agree with him that we are brothers. We must be reconciled. After all, Jesus said that the effectiveness of our efforts in following Him would be directly reflected by our love for one another (John 13:34-35).

15
God's Standard
The Lord's Prayer

In the sixth chapter of Matthew, Jesus provided a model prayer. It has come to be known as the Lord's Prayer. In fact, it is the disciple's prayer because it was requested by them and was given to them. As I said earlier, it is good practice to pray this prayer, daily. Modify the details to fit your circumstances. When I get to the part that is about forgiveness, I pray something like this, "Father, teach us to forgive the way we need to be forgiven. Teach us to forgive *immediately, completely* and *without condition*. Father, please forgive us the way we forgive."

When I pray this, tears often come to my eyes for three reasons. *First*, I remember what it took for Christ to forgive me. He gave all so that I could be free. He literally died to make a way for me to be forgiven. I certainly do not deserve this on any level.

Second, I know that I have failed in this area so many times. This day I have delayed my forgiveness for a number of selfish reasons. Today I have chosen to not forget the wrong done to me by coworkers. There is no excuse for me to be waiting for those unbelievers to ask for forgiveness, but I certainly have been. I know better. I am writing a book on forgiveness, yet I have not passed on the mercy and grace that I have received. If I need this daily reminder to forgive, maybe you do too.

Third, I know that He is going to give me many opportunities this day to get this right. Remember, Jesus came to this planet and was offended at every point. Had He wanted to, He could

15 God's Standard, The Lord's Prayer

have exacted revenge on all of them for their vileness. However, He actively forgave those who sinned against Him in favor of relating to them. Relationship was the goal of His trip. God recognized that Jesus would need to suffer in many ways so that we could know Him.

The responsibility of making God known to a lost and dying world has been passed on to His followers. We now have the job of acting like Jesus acted so that the world might understand that He loves them. Forgiveness is a huge part of this. God allows people to offend us so that we can transmit His forgiveness to them in an observable way. The invisible God wants to use you and me to make Him visible for those who cannot see Him. Will you take up this challenge and begin to actively forgive them today?

The Lord's Prayer is purposely worded the way it is to remind us that the checkpoint for forgiveness from our sins is wrapped up in how we forgive others. We regularly ask God to forgive us in the same way that we forgive others. This is a dangerous request in the light of our track record. We really need help. We would do well to ask for it.

In my experience, we generally are deficient in three ways. *First*, we wait to forgive. *Next,* we forgive only partially. *Lastly,* we forgive with conditions. Each of these stands in opposition to the forgiveness that we expect to receive. This is a contradiction that will do us a lot of harm. I often feel like I am forced to forgive against my will, and I chafe severely at this. I need to remember that I am setting the tone of how I will be forgiven in the future. If I want to be cheerfully forgiven and released from my wrongdoings, I need to model this ahead of time.

This brings up the other issue in the wording of this prayer. The issue is: My behavior in forgiving now, will determine if and how I will be forgiven in the future. What if I do not feel like forgiving, now? This is another passage that seems to fly in the face of my Calvinistic bent. It would be good to read chapter 11 again (pp. 90-95).

16
Five Steps of Forgiveness

When I was very new to the ministry, I was challenged to go far beyond the usual ministerial goal of trying to persuade people to do the right things. I was dared to tell them how.[7] I have tried to not just tell people that they *ought* to do something; I have endeavored to tell them *how*. Forgiveness has been woefully inadequate in this area. Six years ago, when my mother introduced me to the secular study I mentioned before that provided nine steps in the process of forgiveness, I realized that I had failed my students in this. I had been very hard in my teaching about the *need* to forgive, but I had not specified *how* to forgive.

The secular study was trying to design a method to forgive without the power of the sacrifice of Christ. As I said, their first

---
[7] Howard Hendricks was the first one to confront me with this principle. This was in one of his teachings on motivation, which he recorded in the mid-seventies.

step was the same as the one I am proposing. However, after that, they did very little to help with true forgiveness. Their last step was like the last step in this book, but woefully inadequate and humanistic in nature.

I offer the following steps (of forgiveness) not as one who has in any way arrived or as one who has all the answers. I am simply a starving man who can see where the food is. All I am doing is pointing the way with a frail finger. Please join me as I *practice* these steps, in order to someday be like my Savior. In the following steps, it is my prayer that we will be able to know what the mileposts are and follow them.

Step One
Focus on the Offense

This step revolves around describing the offense in graphic detail. There is no shortcut in this step. It has been said that a person is not fully forgiven until they have been fully accused.[8] When required, write out the story of the offense on paper. Do not spare the trees, either. Write as much detail as you can remember. Write about the ramifications of the offense. This includes possible ramifications for you and others. The reason that this is so important is because of our brain's defensive mechanisms. One of these is memory loss.

If an event is too traumatic or painful, the human mind is able to block it out in order to mask the pain. This seems to be an aid in recovery. When we choose to deal with the forgiveness side of the equation, however, there must be full reckoning. The reason for this is because the memory of the offense will come back in the future. Memories come back when the offended person thought he or

---
8 Richard Thompson told me this when I shared part of this process with him. He was and still is a dear friend and colleague.

Section 2 More Blessed to Forgive

she had already forgiven the offense. When this happens, the process of forgiveness will need to be repeated. Since the process of forgiveness can take some time and is not pleasant, the offended person may opt to not ever fully forgive when a new memory surfaces.

For this reason, it is vitally important that we do not skip or diminish this step in any way. The enemy would have us stay in bitterness and resentment, never fully knowing the peace that accompanies full forgiveness. We must not allow memories of offenses to hide in the deep recesses of our minds. We must shine the light of truth on them and fully forgive.

Another reason that may keep us from fully forgiving is that of overlooking an offense. While this is ideal in very petty offenses like a child occasionally acting like a brat, most offenses are not really overlooked when we think they have been. They are buried. The problem with burying the hatchet is that the victim actually wants to bury it in the offender's head. Also, it is always buried alive. It will come up again, in a bigger, different form. Ken Sande's book, *The Peacemaker*,[9] is helpful on this subject.

Another reason that is given to keep from fully exposing the offense is believing that the truth will hurt someone. This is especially true in the case of crimes that are perpetrated against children. Often the offender is a friend or family member that may experience public humiliation or even prison. For this reason, the full story is not ever told, and the offended person is encouraged to forget. I once read that "men forget, but do not forgive; while women forgive, but do not forget."[10] This may be true, but both need to eventually do both.

Remember, this step should not be skipped or taken lightly. The full story and consequences must be enumerated. Take the

---

9 Ken Sande, *The Peacemaker: A Biblical Guide to Resolving Personal Conflict*, Second Edition (Grand Rapids, MI: Baker Books, 1997).
10 Robert Jordan, *The Dragon Reborn (Wheel of Time, Book 3)* (New York, NY: Tor Books, 1991).

16 Five Steps of Forgiveness

time to do this right. By the way, do your best to keep this information to yourself in light of the Matthew 18 instructions. You must keep it between you and your brother for reconciliation purposes.

Step Two
Give the Offense and the Offender to Christ

One of the best things in my life is leading small group discussions and Bible studies. I really love to lead people in their discovery of the Word of God. I love to lead them through the Word of God to meet the God of the Word. I love to train others to lead in these discovery discussions, as well. However, I have found that some of the most common answers have the most potential to end discussions.

Much of the time I spend in these discussions involves questions and answers. I ask questions, expecting thoughtful answers. When I receive a "Sunday School Answer" (I call them this because they are boring and not thought out), I get annoyed. Some of the offensive answers are, Jesus, God, and the Bible. Some of my former students have had vivid memories of my negative reactions to these answers. I am surprised to have to admit that this step two is remarkably similar to one of these annoying answers.

There is no better way to say it than to say it simply. **Give the offense to Jesus Christ**. After all, He paid for it with His own blood. He paid for yours and mine, as well. I hope my former students do not hold this one against me. They will have to forgive me, just this once. There is no better way to say it. Give Jesus your hurts, your cares, your bitterness, your anger, your deformities, and

Section 2 More Blessed to Forgive

your suffering. He really cares for you! Give the IOU for the offense to Him and let it go. He wants to cast it all as far as the east is from the west into the deepest sea to be remembered no more (Micah 7:19; Psalm 103:12). He has done this with your sins. He wants to do this with your bitterness over other people's sins too.

Under the direction of the Holy Spirit, I forcefully spoke these words from the pulpit of a century old church one Sunday morning. Suddenly, people on both sides of the aisle began to weep. I was new to that congregation, so I did not have a clue why. I finished the sermon. A young woman took me to a back office and filled me in on what was going on with the tears. Through her own tears she told me the story. About two years prior to that day, a tragedy had unfolded in the sanctuary where I had just preached.

This young woman was dating a young man and decided to break it off because she was uneasy about his character. Both she and the young man were related to many members of that church. She was a singer in the church and regularly sang a duet with an older man in the church. The two of them were rehearsing one Saturday afternoon in preparation for a special song scheduled for the next day. The jilted young man entered the sanctuary with a loaded 45-caliber handgun, intending to harm her.

He pointed the gun at the young woman and pulled the trigger at point blank range. The gun misfired. He pointed the gun at the older man and pulled the trigger, the gun misfired, again. He pointed the gun at the floor and pulled the trigger, the gun fired. He walked out to the front porch and shot himself in the head. His life ended on the steps of the church. His family blamed the young woman for his death. Her family blamed the young man for the emotional trauma she had endured. Everyone in the church was on one side or the other. The two sides had started to hate each other.

Onto this stage comes little old me with my message of radical obedience to the forgiveness directives of Christ. That night, after some group counseling, I realized that the two sides were

16 Five Steps of Forgiveness

willing to reject the hate and bitterness, but they did not know how. I cried out in anguish on their behalf to my boss, and He gave me this second step. When I told the congregation, they almost laughed. It seemed so very simple. Some of them tried it and began to sleep better. They told their friends and by the next week the previously palpable rift in the church had vanished.

Sadly, this story was just the tip of the proverbial iceberg with respect to bitterness in this congregation. There was a culture of bitterness that had grown up over generations. They believed that the healing that had happened in the case of the shooting could not happen on any other level. They stopped the process, and the Lord could do no more with their group. The old stone building is still there, in the center of that small town, but the flicker of the Spirit that the Lord was fanning had been extinguished.

Step Three
Thank God for the Offense

When I was in Navy boot camp, I had the privilege of serving on a crack rifle squad. We would spin and toss our rifles around with apparent ease. Several of the maneuvers that we performed were a little bit dangerous. In order to keep the injuries to a minimum, the Navy instructors employed a series of tests or inspections that were called checkpoints. These checkpoints were designed to let the instructor know that we were on target in our training and that we were less likely to hurt each other.

There is a very important and telling checkpoint in the process of forgiveness. It is step three. **When you are able to joyfully find a reason to thank God for the offense, you are well on your**

Section 2 More Blessed to Forgive

way to full forgiveness. Notice that I did not say that we should thank God in spite of the offense, or even thank God in the offense. I wrote that we must find a reason to thank God **for** the offense. Remember, God is the creator and sustainer of the universe. Nothing surprises Him. Nothing thwarts His perfect plan for your life. He saw the offense coming. He wants to use it for your good because He really loves you. There will be more on this subject in the chapter on forgiveness and suffering (chapter 18).

My first encountered with this principle was when I was on my first missionary excursion. Fresh out of high school, I thought that I could go to the mission field and spend the rest of my life in missionary service. I moved to Bangkok, Thailand to live and work with my grandparents who were career missionaries. At the time, my grandfather was a high-level official with a multi-national relief agency. He and his staff were assisting Southeast Asian refugees during the Viet Nam War. Even though the U.S. had departed from the war, his work continued for several more years.

During one of our many trips, I had a chance to talk to one of the aide workers who was an American woman in her early twenties. I quickly discerned that she had left home to escape something in her past. I had noticed that she was a little prickly when the subject of men came up. She did not seem to consider me in that category, probably due to my youth. After much prying, I finally found out that she had been raped as a teen and had run from the United States to escape that kind of man (the white kind).

After helping her to see the need to forgive him (I felt inadequate even having *that* conversation), she began to see that her bitterness was only hurting her. She said she would pray about it. I let the subject drop. A few weeks later, we were on another trip. I tactlessly asked what she had decided. She shocked herself by saying that she would try to forgive him.

She then told me that she had said that she would pray about it previously so that I would not bring it back up again. When I did bring it up again, she prayed and asked the Lord to take the

16 Five Steps of Forgiveness

bitterness for the offense away. In fact, she proceeded to do this on the spot, in front of me. Needless to say, it was an intense prayer.

A few days later, she asked me why she was feeling like she had wasted her life since the rape. I quickly shot a prayer up and asked for wisdom. I then asked her what her most memorable moments were since she began as an aide worker. She quickly responded that she had been used in mighty ways when comforting the women refugees who had suffered abuse at the hands of men.

It then dawned on me that the Lord was using her pain to comfort others. This was a reason for her to thank God for the offense that she had suffered. She had not wasted those years but spent them in the most powerful way she possibly could. I later found the passage that speaks about the importance of passing comfort along to others (II Corinthians 1:3-5).

Those refugees could not hear comfort from the Lord in their suffering. They did not know the Lord or His Voice. That young aide worker did have comfort from the Lord. God wanted her to pass His comfort on to them. That was why she was there in Thailand in the first place. Once she saw this truth, her whole life exploded in effectiveness. I never saw her have another down moment. She came to life. Find a reason to thank God for your hurt, and you will find new life too.

Since I first wrote this chapter, I have had some pushback from some of my colleagues in the helping professions. They said that what I am proposing could easily lead to all kinds of dangerous syndromes and disorders. I agree that denying or somehow diminishing the offense can lead to all kinds of interpersonal and mental problems. This is why step one is so very important. However, step 3 is also just as important. In fact, there is powerful Biblical evidence that joy is a godly reaction to the most heinous of crimes.

In Hebrews 12:2b, the writer gave this description of the Lord Jesus Christ, *"For the joy set before him he endured the cross, scorning its shame, and sat down at the right hand of the throne of God."*

Section 2 More Blessed to Forgive

Think of it, the creator and sustainer of the universe, knowing that He would need to be the victim of such an unthinkable crime, considered it pure joy. How could He have this reaction? He knew the final result of our rescue from the slave market of sin was coming. How could my friend in Thailand rejoice because of what had happened to her? She saw many women find the peace of Christ in their horrible circumstances. She shared the comfort that the Lord gave her after the crime she endured.

I know that this is very hard to hear. Please believe that it has been very hard to say for all these years. However, since I have seen the Lord work through this and other counter-intuitive processes over the past four decades, I say it. I say trust the Lord in this, and you will not be disappointed.

By the way, for all of us who cannot imagine how the Lord could produce joy through such heinous acts, let us not forget the principle of individual grace. This Biblical principle states that God gives grace to those who need it, when they need it, for as long as they need it. By way of practical application, He gives grace for us to endure what we endure.

Step Four
Forgive During the Offense

I have lived most of my childhood as a PK. For those of you who are uninitiated in the lingo of churchdom, that stands for Preacher's Kid. As such, I was witness to some ungodly activities perpetrated against my father over the years. There seems to be no end to the stories I have heard from PK's on this subject. Church people can be very unkind when they want to be. When I became a pastor myself, I found that I was not immune to misuse.

Several years ago, I found myself in yet another of these situations. I had been in the process of transitioning a small rural

16 Five Steps of Forgiveness

church from their long-term departing pastor to another, unspecified leadership condition. My team and I did not know at that time whether or not the congregation would even persevere as a local congregation.

Several months into this process, I was in the pulpit, delivering my Sunday morning sermon, when a woman who felt that she was the *real* leader of the church stood up. She began to offer some anecdotal evidence to help prove the point I was making. This was (and still is) not acceptable behavior, even for a backwoods, country church. This was not the first time this had happened in the few months that I had been at that church. My usual response was to finish my sermon abruptly and go home, in anger.

Instead, this time I forgave her on the spot and told her to sit down. My tone over the next few minutes was parental. I gave very specific instructions to that woman and others from the pulpit. There was no anger or malice of any kind in my heart, I simply felt that they were acting like unruly children, and they needed the firm treatment of a loving father. They blew up with excitement. I later remembered that unruly children are often relieved when wrangled (disciplined). They knew that something from the Lord was happening, and they wanted in on it.

The congregation began to grow, and I was able to identify a young man in their midst as their next pastor. A few months later, I installed him as such and was able to move on from there with a good sense about their future. None of this would have happened if I had not stopped my usual response when church people act poorly. Instead, I followed the directive of step four in the process of forgiveness and forgave *during* the offense.

This step is for chronic or habitual offenses that never seem to end. It is also needed when the pain of the offense lasts a long time. We should never forget the prayer of Jesus when He was hanging on the cross, "Father, forgive them, for they know not what they are doing." We would do well to imitate Him in this.

Section 2 More Blessed to Forgive

When Peter asked Jesus if it would be enough for him to forgive his brother for the same offense, seven times a day, he must have been shocked at what Jesus answered. Peter must have had some person in mind, like Andrew (his brother). He must have had some offense in mind. He must have previously done the tabulation in his head concerning the time it would take for Andrew to commit that offense seven times to know it would fill a whole day.

Factoring in the time it takes to apologize and the time for make-up hugs, the number seven seemed to represent most of their waking hours. Jesus, then, blew all that out of the water by a factor of seventy. This was *absurdly impossible*. However, the point was made that there needs to be forgiveness **during** all this offending.

Jesus suffered on the Cross and modeled this step for all to see. He prayed for the Father to forgive them. This whole statement was offered in the form of a prayer. He asked the Father to forgive them for they did not know what they were doing. The point of this story for the purpose of forgiveness is the fact that He forgave and pleaded on someone's behalf while He was being tortured. It is impossible to imagine the grace required for such an act of mercy.

The first martyr for the cause of Christ, Stephen, prayed a similar prayer during the offense that sent him to Heaven. An angry mob rushed at him in their fury and began to pummel him with stones. Knowing this was the end, this godly deacon restated Christ's prayer and forgave his murderers. It is one thing to imagine that our Lord and King is faithful to do what He came for (to forgive us). It is quite another to see a lowly deacon repeating this act of mercy. The fact that the future apostle Paul (Saul) was in that angry crowd brings new light to the need for this step.

Saul was an up-and-coming Pharisee who was about to embark on a prolonged mission to eradicate the Early Church. He was part of the group that chased followers of Jesus Christ out of the city of Jerusalem and into other cities. This was no small feat of dedication for a young Jew of his day. There was an inherent

16 Five Steps of Forgiveness

danger assigned to Jews with this calling on their life. They were subject to far too much interaction with Gentiles. This, in turn, could lead to their own defilement and cast them from their station in life. However, Saul was willing to take this risk. He could sleep at night in the knowledge that these heretic followers of Christ were not allowed to exist.

Saul was a witness, on the day Stephen was stoned. He was also a witness to this man's response to such treatment. Stephen did not rail against his attackers. Rather, he prayed for them to be forgiven. This uncharacteristic response must have marked Saul, who was later to become the apostle Paul for the rest of his life. The evidence of this mark on his life was the fact that the same scenario of potential martyrdom was perpetrated against him many times in his life. His response was always the same, forgiveness.

Step Five
Change Your Version of the Offense From Victim to Victor

There is evidence that self-talk has enormous value. The idea behind this concept is that what a person says to himself is weighty and pushes him to action. A top athlete that tells himself that he is going to win the championship is much more likely to do so than the one who feels that he does not belong on the field of play. Of course, Solomon said it best when he said, *"As a man thinks in his heart, so is he"* (Proverbs 23:7). My favorite version of this was spoken by one of my mentors this way, "You are not what you think you are. What you think, you are."[11]

One of the best ways to solidify forgiveness is to overhaul the story of the offense. The story had previously included some

---

11 Dr. Howard Hendrick: I followed his ministry from the time I was 11 years old until his death a few years ago. This world is a little less since his passing. May his tribe increase!

Section 2 More Blessed to Forgive

elements of a bad person doing something unthinkable. In this story, we were the victims. The other people were the hostile perpetrators. In step 5, we simply change the story.

The new story needs to stop the victim-like words. There needs to be a victor in the new story. Even though the perpetrator (that bad person who did bad things) offended us, we were able to overcome. Then, we victoriously rose above the offense to forgive. The story does not stop at this point. The real power behind your ability to forgive was Christ's finished work on the Cross. He paid the price for that offense. He helped you to realize the incredible need to forgive. He is the real victor in the new story. It is astonishing how powerful this new story can be.

In the 1950's a young, skinny, country preacher traveled to New York to reach the gangs in that city with the Gospel of Jesus Christ. He finally found and confronted the leader of one of the gangs with the message of Jesus' love and mercy. This leader's name was Nicky Cruz.

Nicky's initial response to this message was to threaten the evangelist, David Wilkerson, with a knife. He also slapped Wilkerson in the face. Wilkerson's reaction was to tell that young thug that even if he were to cut him in a thousand pieces, every piece would say that Jesus loved him.[12] This was a clear message of forgiveness for the slap. When Nicky Cruz became aware that Christ had forgiven him, his reaction was to fall on his knees in repentance and accept Jesus as his Savior. The Lord communicated His love and forgiveness through Wilkerson to Cruz.

Jesus wants to do this through you, as well. Have you ever wondered why you had to go through all the heartaches and pain? This is the age-old question of why a good God could allow bad things to happen to good people. I am not in the place of God. I do not even pretend to understand all the answers to this question. However, one reason for suffering is the transmittal of God's grace

---

12 Wilkerson, David and John and Elizabeth Sherrill, *The Cross and the Switchblade*, (New York, NY: Bernard Geis Associates, 1963).

16 Five Steps of Forgiveness

to a lost and dying world. After all, Jesus had to suffer for this. Would it not be perfectly reasonable for the Lord to continue the transmittal of His grace through you? He can do this most effectively when you forgive.

His older brothers treated the patriarch Joseph very badly. Their father, Jacob, clearly loved Joseph more than his ten older brothers. This made them resentful of Joseph. They had a bad case of jealousy. Some of them could have been middle aged when they took aggressive action against the teenager, Joseph. They threw him in a well. Some of them intended to kill him later. Instead, they sold him into slavery. This led to time in servitude and time in jail for Joseph. On the home front, Joseph's father grieved because he was led to believe that a wild animal had killed Joseph.

All of this finally led to the exaltation of Joseph to the second highest post in the most powerful nation on earth. The Lord caused this to happen in order to save many people from an imminent, widespread famine. Some of the people who needed salvation from this famine were his older brothers and family. They were all saved through the famine. After their father, Jacob, died years later, his older brothers thought Joseph may still be planning his revenge.

They came to him and asked for his forgiveness, sort of. Actually, they pleaded with him to not kill them in revenge. This request grieved Joseph. He responded through his tears with the most profound statement of faith and forgiveness, "You intended to harm me, but God intended it for good to accomplish what is now being done, the saving of many lives" (Genesis 50:20).

This is exactly the kind of heart the Lord is looking for in His children. He allows bad things to happen to us, for the salvation of many. When we extend love and forgiveness to those who harm us, we reach people. They find Christ. He forgives them and they join the family of God. (More on this in chapter 20.) The awesome truth is that our forgiveness story is the key that unlocks this powerful dynamic of evangelism.

17

Forgiving Yourself

There is an insidious tendency of some people to let everyone off the proverbial hook except themselves. The origin of this seems to be rooted in the idea that once we are forgiven of a lifestyle of sin, we are obligated to "sin no more." We say something like, "Now that I have been forgiven, I must live a perfect life. After all, does not the Bible say that we are to be perfect, just as our heavenly Father is perfect?" (See Matthew 5:48) Under this logic, many abuses have been justified.

Jesus told the story that I mentioned earlier of the servant who was forgiven of a great debt. As you may recall, he promptly went out and launched a debt collection campaign. He did this because he did not believe the king really forgave him, or maybe he thought that he was still able to pay the debt. It does not matter why; the fact is that he had no hope of paying it back. The person (King) who held the marker had forgiven the debt. The root of this servant's bad response to forgiveness was pride. The servant in this story did not want to be forgiven; he wanted to pay his own way.

Pride is the root of perfectionism. We honestly believe that we can earn all we need for our existence. This is contrary to the Gospel of Jesus Christ. It is only when we discover and embrace our inadequacy that we can find rest for our souls. The first point of the Gospel is the realization that we are sinful. This sinful state leads to death. The only remedy for this is the death of Jesus Christ on the cross and personal acceptance of His sacrifice. Perfectionism says the opposite of this.

Perfectionism leads us to deny our own inadequacy in place of humanistic pride. I have met many churchgoers who actually

17 Forgiving Yourself

embrace this as their lifestyle. They couch this vanity in sanctimonious rhetoric to disguise their duplicity. They may say, something like, "If it is worth doing it is worth doing right." Or "We must be excellent in what we do." Or "God commanded that we be perfect as He is perfect." (A better translation of Matthew 5:48 would be *holy* rather than *prefect*). If I have just described you, I beg you to see the truth about yourself and reject perfectionism as sin.

On the other hand, some of you are not willing to let go of what you have done. You have convinced yourself that all other sins are forgivable except yours. You may even be able to forgive this same sin in the life of another person, but not in your life. I have found that the particular sin that plagues a particular demographic is sexual sin. This category of sin usually haunts women. Not that men are not just as guilty, but women seem to feel it more.

What you need to know is that you are forgiven. Jesus died for *that* sin. He died for all the details of *that* sin and any residual guilt associated with it. When He was dying on the Cross, He had *that* sin in mind. He bought the marker on a cosmic level for *that* sin. He has sent it as far as the east is from the west. He will remember it no more.

Are you willing to join your king in this forgetfulness? After all, who are you to disagree with the creator and sustainer of the universe? You must decide in your heart to totally rely on *His* perfection. *His* goodness needs to be the focus on your life, not *yours*. This is basic to following Christ. I know this may be hard to swallow. However, these are the very words of life. You need to embrace them with all your heart.

As I mentioned before, my father was successful as a Christian counselor for some years. During his time in this capacity, he had the opportunity to meet Amy. (Let us call her that.) Amy was a beautiful woman in her thirties who was suffering from what we now call obsessive-compulsive disorder. She had been

Section 2 More Blessed to Forgive

seeing several professional therapists for a decade and a half when she met my dad. In case my previous description of my dad's style was unclear, he was a very direct communicator. He also was only interested in getting to the bottom of any problem that he faced. For several weeks, he allowed Amy to tell her story, without much interference.

Amy lived alone after several serious relationships had failed. She was desperately lonely and acutely felt the need to find her soul mate. However, she had abruptly ended the most promising relationships without any good reasons. She had a number of quirks in her daily routine. One of these was glaring because of its persistent regularity.

Every night, before going to bed, Amy would lock the doors to her house. After getting into her bed, she would hear, almost audibly, an accusing voice telling her that she forgot to lock the doors. She would get out of bed and check the doors to make sure they were locked. This would happen several times per night. Eventually, she would be able to convince the voice that she did not believe that the doors were unlocked. She would fall into a fitful sleep, afraid that the doors were unlocked.

This scenario did not seem reasonable to my father. He began to probe further until he discovered when this obsession began. He found that it had been happening all her adult life. In fact, it began when she was a senior in high school. A few weeks before this obsession began, Amy had engaged in a sexual sin that she thoroughly enjoyed. She began to feel guilty, not only because she committed the sin, but also because she enjoyed it. She decided to make a deal with whoever was making her feel guilty. The deal was that she would live a perfect life if she did not have to deal with that one sin. She was convinced that she would be able to live this perfect life in order to atone for that sin.

The voice that was accusing her of the sin of not locking the doors had found one thing that she was unsure of and exploited it.

17 Forgiving Yourself

Upon hearing this story, my father led Amy to the understanding that Jesus died for all sin, including that sexual sin that Amy had committed. That day, Amy gave up on the sinful lifestyle of perfectionism. That night, she locked her doors once and went to sleep. She was married soon thereafter. Sadly, her husband died a few years later.

As a young sailor, I befriended Amy a few years after that in a mid-western city. I found her to be a strong and confident person. Soon after this I was assigned to another location, and we parted ways. She married again and has since been living as the happy mother of several children. All the vestiges of her disorder have been gone for decades. All she needed to do was renounce her perfectionism and embrace Christ's forgiveness for her sin.

If this story reminds you of a story in your own life, you should know that there is a great deal of hope for you. God really loves perfectionists. They have a kindred spirit to Him. He loves their desire for order and justice. However, the perfectionist must also understand that there is only one God. He truly is the only perfect being in His universe. He is also a jealous God. He does not share His position with anyone. If you are still bent toward striving for absolute perfection, please realize that you have a big problem.

The Bible says that God resists the proud. He also gives grace to the humble. Since you have read this, you are at a crossroad in your life. You must choose to reject your overwhelming craving for perfection. This is simply pride in the face of a holy God. This pride comes from the evil one and is sin. This leads to death. The other option is to accept the free gift of God's forgiveness through Jesus' atoning sacrifice. This choice leads to life—-abundant life. Please, choose this one.

18
Forgiveness and Suffering

The more time I spend on this planet, walking with the Lord, the more I have become convinced of some things. *First*, the Christian walk is marked with suffering. Our first call after the one to follow Christ is to suffer. Numerous times Jesus said that the person who would follow Him effectively would need to take up and carry his cross. If the cross is not a load of suffering, I do not know what is. Jesus, as the Master, suffered. He assured His disciples that they would suffer, as well. These men all suffered greatly for the cause of Christ. Throughout the stages and periods of church history, those who would live godly lives have suffered. John Foxe's little *Book of Martyrs* is filled with the suffering of Christ's disciples.[13]

The *second* fact that I have come to discover about this subject is that the most painful suffering comes at the hands of other people. It is one thing to suffer during a natural catastrophe along with all the other victims. It is quite another to be a victim of a violent crime. It is one thing to suffer during an accident of some sort. It is quite another to suffer rejection and violence at the hands of a person that was once close to us.

Third, we must not forget the probability that the enemy of our souls is very interested in causing our destruction. Failing this, he and his minions are often busy causing much suffering in humanity. Followers of Christ are not only susceptible to the general havoc that is wreaked upon humans, but we are also some of the enemy's special targets. A casual read-through of the ancient story of Job will drive this point home.

---
13 John Foxe, *Book of Martyrs*, John Day, 1563.

18 Forgiveness and Suffering

When we consider how the subject of forgiveness factors into suffering, the focus needs to center on the second of these suffering sources. People are often the cause of our suffering. Whether they intend it or not, when two sinful people are in proximity with each other, one or both of them will experience suffering. Grace is required if a relationship is to be endured. Most conflicts among individuals may be avoided if we are willing to be gracious in the face of suffering. There is, of course a fine line between the need to overlook an offense and excusing an offense that needs to be acknowledged and forgiven.

The person who has been offended needs to determine if the offense is too big to be overlooked. All but the lowest levels of offense usually dictate that the forgiveness process must be initiated. In these cases, the process should be worked through in spite of feelings. Some of these include offenses that affect more than one person, offenses that require restitution, and offenses that are considered crimes by an impartial authority. This is not an exhaustive list and may be expanded.

Section 2 More Blessed to Forgive

19
The Other Side of Forgiveness

There is an abundant life that is free for the taking. Jesus talked of it often. It is available to all who will walk in His light and follow Him. It comes after we commit to obedience in areas of our life that we do not naturally feel able. One of these is the area of forgiveness. Abundant life is on the other side of forgiveness. In fact, we will never really know the fullness of the abundant life that Jesus talked about until we forgive from our heart.

One summer I met Aria (not her real name). She was working as an intern in a ministry that has an impact in a major city in America. A good Christian family raised her in rural Pennsylvania. When she was young, her grandmother contracted a fatal illness. In the months before her grandmother's death, Aria begged her parents to be allowed to see her grandmother once more before she died. She even went so far as to beg God, in prayer, to be able to say goodbye. In spite of this, she did not see her grandmother in time. She had never forgotten or forgiven her family for this loss.

19 The Other Side of Forgiveness

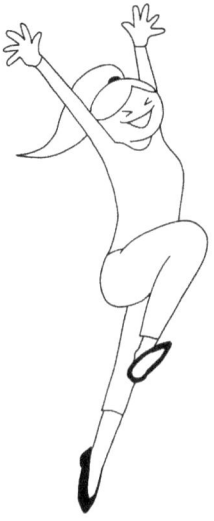

    I met her as a young adult when she arrived at the ministry for service. I briefly explained some of the principles surrounding forgiveness. Several days later, she experienced a spiritual renewal. She gave the IOU for the debt she held against her parents to Christ. After this she began to blossom into the woman that God had always wanted her to be. Her team and I were so very excited to watch her in this process.

    The abundant life that she has entered into is available for you, too. God wants to deliver you from all that garbage, in favor of life, a life that is controlled by the Holy Spirit. Will you choose this life today? I assure you from the bottom of my heart, there is no better way to live.

20
The Evangelistic Challenge

I was once challenged to condense the outward, visible indicators of followers of Christ into one over-arching principle or characteristic. We say that we are different, and we belong to God. (This is a very good definition of holiness, at least on the personal level.) However, when outsiders look at us, they see characteristics that are not too far removed from their own. They often simply do not see much difference between themselves and us.

For example, some people of Hebrew descent call us Sunday people. This contrasts their view of themselves, Saturday people. What they are asserting is that they worship God on Saturday, and we worship our misled version of Him on Sunday. Could this be most of what outsiders see as our distinctive? If this is so, we are not faithfully communicating the Good News. If all we are is a people who meet on a particular day of the week, as opposed to other people who meet on another day, then our message is religious at its core. It does not matter what information is disseminated at those meetings, the fact that the **meetings are our distinctive to outsiders** sends the wrong message to them.

What I am asking is similar to the first of two questions that the Lord asked His disciples in Matthew 16 beginning in verse 13. He asked them who people said that He was. This question was important because it identified the message that was actually being received by the target audience. The answer that the disciples provided indicated a certain level of effectiveness in their communication. From the context, the Lord did not want the outside world to know that He was the Messiah at that time (Verse 20).

20 The Evangelistic Challenge

In light of their response, Jesus could conclude that the communication of His being *anything* but the Messiah was effective (Verse 14). We need to ask specific questions to the outside world concerning the message that they are receiving in order to gauge the effectiveness of our message. By the way, a big part of our current message needs to include the fact that Jesus *is* the Messiah, the One sent to the world by Almighty God.

Followers of Christ are benevolent, giving people in general. Nowhere in the Gospels is it recorded that it is more blessed to give than to receive. However, the apostle Paul quoted Christ as saying these words. (See Acts 20:35.)

One of the greatest gifts that we can give is forgiveness. We need to learn to extend the forgiveness of Christ to individuals that offend us. This does not mean that we act like doormats and "overlook" their offenses. We need to learn to be offended at what our Master finds offensive, yes, but we also need to listen to Him when He indicates that we are in a vital spiritual moment in a person's life. We need to show our offense in clear yet kind ways. Then, just as visibly forgive them. How this looks will be different with each of you, in each situation.

When we are able to transmit Christ's forgiveness in this way, we might win them to Him and His kingdom. This powerful dynamic is missing from our arsenal of soul-winning strategies. The evangelistic challenge is to prayerfully use it for the furtherance of the Kingdom. There are many sinners out there who have never seen forgiveness modeled. I am confident that when they do, they will make haste to enter into our family.

Section 2 More Blessed to Forgive

21
Questions and Answers

Question: What if the offense against me is not clearly sin?

Answer: Forgive the offense as if it were sin and let the Lord convict the offender for his behavior or words.

Question: What if a believer will not forgive me? I am not even sure what I did to offend her. I have asked her and she says there is nothing, but she is clearly offended about something.

Answer: When a person has a root of bitterness, her demeanor toward everyone and everything changes. There is a possibility that she is simply angry with someone else for a specific offense and just *seems* angry with you. However, this information only helps you cope and is more like a Band-Aid on a tumor. Since this person is not forgiving someone, it is safe to say that she is not forgiven, based on the Matthew 6 passage. So, act like she is an unbeliever and win her over to Christ. As much as lies within you, live at peace with her. Ken Sande's book, *The Peacemaker,* would be of some help with this one.[14]

---

14 Ken Sande, *The Peacemaker: A Biblical Guide to Resolving Personal Conflict*, Second Edition, (Grand Rapids, MI: Baker Books, 1997).

21 Questions and Answers

Question: What if her feelings are just hurt because I yelled at her, I did no wrong as far as a sinful act?

Answer: Treat the incident as a sinful act because you were unkind. Act as though you did a sinful act and let the Lord sort it out. Remember that the goal is reconciliation. Again, Ken Sande's book would probably be helpful here, too.[15]

Question: What if a person has tried all this and the feelings of bitterness have stayed around?

Answer: We must not rule out the fact that we are at war on this earth. There really is a devil, and he is very motivated to destroy the followers of Christ. Since we have chosen to follow Jesus even when He is walking on the water, we must come to grips with the supernatural world. The best book I have read on the subject is *The Bondage Breaker* by Neil Anderson.[16] It is amazing to realize that we have such a powerful enemy, however, our Lord has already overcome him.

---

15   Ibid.

16 Neil T. Anderson, *The Bondage Breaker,* (Eugene, OR: Harvest House Publishers, 2000).

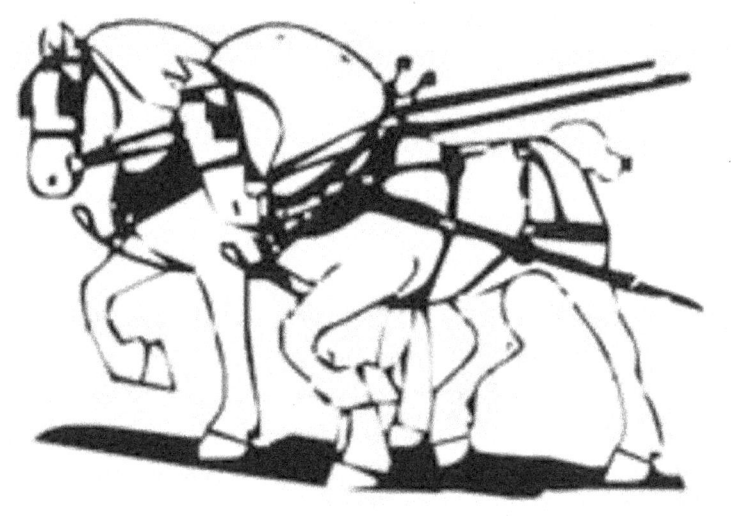

Section Three

Two By Two Leadership

Section 3 Two by Two Leadership

Introduction

The modern church is facing a leadership crisis of epidemic proportion. There are more moral failures and missteps in the personal lives of spiritual leaders than ever in the history of the Christian church. Beyond this, the confidence level of the leaders that survive the onslaught of moral degradation is also at an all-time low. The evidence that the church in the West is quickly slipping into irrelevance is irrefutable.[17] The general state of Christian leadership is **disrepute, disrepair,** and **disempowerment.**

The reputation of the church is in **disrepute**. There are so many examples of this that it almost seems passé to review them. The main reason for this lack of credibility is the lack of perceived integrity of Christian leaders. There are far too many instances of infidelity and deceit extant among those who have occupied the top spots in Christian ministries.[18] It is interesting that many church members see these problems in other churches and not in their own church. It is as if many believe that *other* leaders are not trustworthy, but *their* pastor is above reproach.

The church is in **disrepair**. Even a casual glance at a phone book or online registry will indicate that there are many flavors of the church in any given locality. Far too many of these have found their origins in church conflict. It is as if the very fabric of the church is tearing itself apart. In 1511, Martin Luther posted his 95 theses to mark the beginning of the Reformation—a schism from

---

17 Mark Driscoll, *Confessions of a Reformissional Reverend* (Grand Rapids, MI: Zondervan, 2006), pp. 16-18.

18 Richard J. Krejcir "What is Going on with the Pastors in America?" Schaeffer Institute of Church Leadership Development. Accessed Mar. 2024, http://www.churchleadership.org/apps/articles/default.asp?articleid=42347&columnid=4545.

Catholicism, and schisms have not ceased since.[19] Not only are there new denominations and congregations that have emerged from these splits, but also most churches have internal strife that is almost comical if it were not so sad.[20] The anecdotal illustrations about members fighting over the color of the carpet in the sanctuary are not only proliferated, but they are also fully believable. The church is not only in disrepair due to splits and divisions, but she is also often caught engaged in unproductive activity.[21]

The church is **disempowered**. There is an apathy in America about fulfilling the requirement of the Great Commission, which was given by Christ.[22] The American population is growing steadily while the number of those who claim the Name of Christ has begun to decline.[23] Those in leadership try to put a positive spin on this fact, but the church is not doing what she was created to do, which is to make disciples. Further, the disciples who are being made are not like those in the New Testament. One of the traits of these New Testament disciples was that they stayed busy making even more disciples. There are several indicators pointing to the fact that this is not being done in adequate numbers. "80-85% of churches are plateaued or declining."[24]

---

19 *Michael Tummillo, "Surviving an American Church Split."* Accessed Mar. 2024. http://ezinearticles.com/?Surviving-an-American-Church-Split&id=161200.

20 Alfred Poirier, *The Peace Making Pastor: A Biblical Guide to Resolving Church Conflict* (Grand Rapids, MI: Baker Books, 2006), pp. 9-10.

21 Colin Marshall and Tony Payne, *The Trellis and The Vine: The Ministry Mind-Shift That Changes Everything* (Kingsford NSW, Australia: Matthias Media, 2009), pp. 8-10.

22 Elmer Towns, Ed Stetzer, and Warren Bird, *11 Innovations in the Local Church: How Today's Leaders Can Learn, Discern and Move into the Future* (Ventura, CA: Regal Books, 2007), p. 14.

23 Julia Duin, "Just in: Latest Church Growth Statistics," *The Washington Times*, February 12, 2010. Accessed Mar. 2024. http://www.washingtontimes.com/blog/belief-blog/2010/feb/12/latest-church-growth-stats-in/

24 Aubrey Malphurs, "The State of the American Church: Plateaued or Declining," *The Malphurs Group*, Sept. 5, 2014. Accessed Jun. 2024. https://malphursgroup.com/state-of-the-american-church-plateaued-declining/

Section 3 Two by Two Leadership

One of the reasons for the decline in leadership in the Christian church is that of unrealistic expectations. The modern church requires her leaders to be better than proficient at all aspects of leadership. There is an expectation that the leader must not only be a very spiritual person, but also a motivational speaker and a top executive manager, as well. On this level, the modern Christian leader must wear the proverbial hats of both the chief executive officer and the chief financial officer for the church. He or she must be expertly skilled in all the specialties of modern business leadership models; while finding the resources to hold the hand of the dying member at any given hour of the day or night.

On top of all this, the particular style of leadership, which is employed by the modern Christian leader, must match the preferred style of those individuals that he or she would lead. This expectation is in place even though every individual in a given room expects something different from their leader at any given time. If this were not enough, the Christian leader must maintain a personal household of faith, making time to be the example of how to be the best spouse and parent. The compensation for this is minimal.[25]

In short, the modern Christian leader is not able to meet all the expectations that are placed upon him or her. There is too much to do and not enough resources. The number of disciples being made is abysmal. These facts are known and felt by most Christian leaders on a weekly basis. Because of this, their confidence is gone. The profession of Christian leadership is one of the least self-assured of any demographic.[26] Christian leaders are not doing their job. They cannot do their job, and they know it.

---

25 Chuck Bentley, "A Pastor's Salary," Crown Financial Ministries. Accessed September 14, 2012. http://www.crown.org/library/viewarticle.aspx?articleid=148.

26 Jim Fuller, Pastoral Care Inc., "Statistics in the Ministry." Accessed Mar. 2024., http://www.pastoralcareinc.com/statistics/.

Introduction

There are at least two parts to understanding any problem. The first of these is to well define the problem, and the second is to propose a solution. Philosopher and author, John Dewy (1859-1952), is credited with saying that a "Problem, well-defined is a problem half-solved." What has been discussed thus far is a description of the problem, utilizing sweeping statements and broad parameters. However, a more concise understanding of the dilemma facing the modern church is required before any real progress may be realized.

Three Categories of Problems Facing Christian Leaders Today

First, they are not getting the job done.[27] When the founder of the church (Christ) left, He gave instructions concerning what the goals and objectives of the church should be. These are found in all four Gospels and in the book of Acts (Matthew 28:18-20, Mark 16:15, Luke 24:47, John 20:21, Acts 1:8). It is easy to understand from these passages that the church is supposed to be about the business of making disciples.[28] This (the making of disciples) is to produce an ongoing, growing, healthy church that ultimately reaches every individual on the planet. However, this ideal church is not what is seen today.[29]

Second, as I touched on earlier, there is a plethora of unrealistic expectations placed on the average Christian leader.[30] These seem to come from all stakeholders in and around the church. Those outside the church seem to believe that the church can and should do more to help them in their dizzzzzfficulties. Those inside

---

27 Aubrey Malphurs, *Strategic Planning: A 21st-Century Model For Church And Ministry Leaders*, Grand Rapids, MI: Baker Books, 1999, 2005, 2013.

28 Rick Warren, *The Purpose-Driven Church: Growth Without Compromising Your Message & Mission* (Grand Rapids, MI: Zondervan, 1995), pp 103-107.

29 George Barna, *Growing True Disciples* (Colorado Springs, CO: Water Brook Press, 2001), pp. 85-98.

30 George Barna, *The Power of Team Leadership: Finding Strength in Shared Responsibility* (Colorado Springs, CO: WaterBrook Press, 2001), pp. 1-7.

Section 3 Two by Two Leadership

the church seem to expect their leaders to be all things to all people and meet all *their* needs. The leaders themselves seem to expect to be able to live up to these very demanding standards of excellence and competence in all areas of life and leadership.

Third, there is an undercurrent of instability in the sub-conscious minds of most Christian leaders.[31] Some have labeled this undercurrent, burnout.[32] This may be due to the first two difficulties stated above. It is as though the average leader knows that the job is not getting done. Further, he or she knows that they are not able to fill all the roles which are required to get the job done in the first place. This leads to the third problem of the lack of self-confidence.

These problems have been discussed in a variety of contexts. A variety of culprits have been indicted, from the incompetence and vice of individual leaders to the idea that the average church is too complex.[33] These and other proverbial smoking guns may appeal to some people as being the reasons for the leadership crisis. However, these reasons lack credibility as the real causes.

There is one cause that may seem too simplistic to be credible. However, when contrasted against the problem of the leadership crisis, it may be the right cause. In most cases, under the current model of today's church, there is only one leader at the top.[34] Since it is impossible for any one person to do all the jobs that are required for this role, there is an easy solution.

---

31 Jim Fuller, Pastoral Care Inc., "Statistics in the Ministry,." Accessed Mar. 2024. http://www.pastoralcareinc.com/statistics/.

32 Nicholas W. Twigg and Bomi Kang, "The Effect of Leadership, Perceived Support, Idealism, and Self Esteem on Burnout," *Journal of Behavioral Studies in Business* (April 2011). Accessed Mar. 2024. http://search.proquest.com.ezproxy.liberty.edu:2048/docview/ 928758842.

33 Thom S Rainer and Eric Geiger, *Simple Church: Returning to God's Process for Making Disciples* (Nashville, TN: Broadman & Holman, 2006), pp. 26-27.

34 George Barna, *The Power Of Team Leadership: Achieving Success Through Shared Responsibility* (Colorado Springs, CO: Waterbrooks Press, a division of Random House, Inc. 2001), Chapter 1.

Introduction

There should be more than one person at the top of all Christian organizations. "The key to a fulfilled life is relationships."[35] Rather than a single person filling the role of senior pastor or the equivalent, there should always be a co-pastor situation in the leadership structure of every Christian organization. The solution is not that the modern church needs to find better, more effective leadership; it is that there needs to be a shared leadership role in every situation. "One person alone will never change the whole world."[36]

Some have suggested that the idea of the plurality of leadership is what is needed.[37] However, while it is true that teams always beat individuals, the model that embraces a **team** leadership structure is also doomed to repeat the problems of the current situation. This is because of the nature of leadership. When there are *many* leaders in a committee, for example, nothing gets done until a person emerges as *the* leader of that committee. This is why the first instruction given to a jury is for the members to elect a foreperson. The very real result of the team leadership models is another echelon of bureaucracy. Rather than something getting done by the committee of "leaders," one individual sets the agenda and gets the others on the committee to follow or get off the committee. Therefore, all this model breeds is hierarchical bureaucracy.

The possible solution is to install **partnerships** in leadership in all Christian organizations. This needs to be put into place at the top echelons of these organizations and carried down through all levels. These partnerships need to be publicly known and privately upheld. The individuals who occupy the opposing halves of the partnerships need to be committed to the leadership and ministries of the other half as if the other leader was more important and

---

35 Oscar W. Thompson Jr., *Concentric Circles of Concern: Seven Stages for Making Disciples* (Nashville, TN: Broadman & Holman Publishers, 1999), p. 11.
36 Alvin L. Reid, *Radically Unchurched: Who They Are and How to Reach Them* (Grand Rapids, MI: Kregel Publications, 2002), p. 62.
37 Barna, *The Power Of Team Leadership, pp.* 19-27.

Section 3 Two by Two Leadership

authoritative than themselves. Partner "A" needs to see partner "B" as his or her boss and accountability confidant. Partner "B" needs to see partner "A" as his or her boss and accountability confidant, as well. There is no room for one superseding the other with respect to the question of who is in charge. The only time one may possibly override the other would be in an area of specialization or giftedness.

By the way, I value both genders with respect to leadership. There is no male or female in Christ. However, with respect to genders, I have always felt very strongly that having only same gender teams is the best practice. Men do best when working with men and women with women. I have also found that the husband-wife team is for the family and not for the church.

The solo leader in the local church is a monstrosity. The base of support for this model comes from the felt need of many in leadership to be in total control of the organization. This need has no place in Christian circles. Not that the felt need to be in control is altogether misplaced or that not feeling this need is altogether healthy; but that the need for the leader to feel that he is in total, top leadership control is out of bounds in the Christian experience. The fact is that the Lord Jesus Christ spoke against it (Matt. 20:25-28; Luke 22:25-27). He Himself claimed to be the One in charge. He does not share this responsibility. He declared that He would build His church and the very gates of hell would not prevail against it (Matthew 16:18b). The Lord is very much in control of His church via the agent of the Holy Spirit. And His design for ministry is shared, two by two leadership. He sent his leaders out two by two.

22

Biblical and Historical Foundations

So, the general understanding among Christian leaders today is that there is a crisis in leadership. While many have weighed in on the subject with respect to how this has happened and possible remedies, the problem seems too complex for a quick and easy fix. Now, to fully appreciate the issues that are facing leaders today, a review of the historical background on this matter is essential. This chapter will cover both the Biblical history of shared, two by two leadership and the examples of this model being carried forward into church history.

Section 3 Two by Two Leadership

Biblical History of Leadership Partnerships

So, disciples of Christ in the world today should take narrative accounts of what Christ and His apostles did as examples to followed. On at least three occasions, Jesus sent His disciples into ministry two by two. These were the sending of the twelve, the sending of the seventy-two, and the sending of the two for preparation of the Passover.

In apparent imitation of this, the early church sent apostles out two by two in almost every situation that needed some intervention or leadership. The Holy Spirit for the historic First Missionary journey upheld this policy in the calling and deployment of two leaders, apostles Paul and Barnabas, for this work who were not among the original twelve disciples (Acts 13:1-3). It is interesting that this policy was continued in successive missionary journeys.

Before the beginning of the Second Missionary Journey, there was a disagreement between the leaders of the First Missionary Journey. This resulted in two groups going out in two directions. However, both groups employed the partnership principle when forming their leadership teams (Acts 15:36-41). Paul chose Silas as his partner and Barnabas chose John-Mark. This effectively doubled the potential impact of the Second Missionary Journeys. Although there are no records on the Barnabas leg of this journey, the impact of this journey must have been great on the person of John-Mark because he was transformed from a quitter into a major leader in his own right. He is purported to have written the Gospel of Mark and was later viewed by none other than the apostle Paul (the guy who would not include him on the second journey) as being of help in his (Paul's) last days (II Timothy 4:11).

There is another hermeneutical principle that applies when considering whether a narrative is to be considered normative or

22 Political and Historical Foundations

able to be applied as policy for the church today. If a Biblical author repeats a detail of how a Biblical character operated, the author may be implying that this is something that needs to be imitated.[38] If this is true when examining the writings of a human author, how much more true would this principle be when discussing the combined works of the Holy Spirit? If some act or detail is consistently present in the whole counsel of the Word of God, then this detail must, indeed, be applicable.

Not Good For Man to be Alone

Moses recorded the time God first was not pleased with something (Genesis 2:18). God had made a checklist of sorts at the end of each stage of the development of the universe, and He saw that the parts were good. No less than five times does Moses record that these stages were good in God's sight (Gen. 1:10, 12, 18, 21, 25). If this was not enough, the author of Genesis recorded that God looked over the whole of His creation and declared that it was *very* good (Gen. 1:31). It may be deduced, then, that God was quite pleased with His creation, both the parts and the whole.

It was at this point that the story turned a little bit sour. When examining the account in more detail, Moses recorded in the second chapter that God said that it was not good that man was alone (Gen. 2:18). This contrasting statement of displeasure was designed to show that God had a special place in the society to come for the woman, perhaps in case the man ever lost sight of her importance.

God provided a partner, Eve, to be with Adam, to help him. She was to be the second person who was like the man. All the other animals had two, except man. This was a clear distinctive. All the other animals were created by God's spoken word. They were created from nothing. They were, therefore, just like the rest of the

---

38 William Klein, Craig Blomberg, and Robert Hubbard, *Introduction to Biblical Interpretation* (Nashville, TN: Thomas Nelson, Inc., 2004), pp. 424-426.

Section 3 Two by Two Leadership

creation. Man, however, was formed from the dust of the earth, and God breathed life into his body (Gen. 2:7). This set him apart from all the other created beings. For this reason, the woman had to be made in a special way to set her apart from the rest of creation, as well.

Much has been made of the fact that God utilized one of Adam's ribs from which to form her. The point, for the purposes of this discussion, is that she was special, a necessary part of God's plan for humankind. She was brought to the man so that his aloneness could be alleviated. The first problem presented in the story of humankind was that man was alone and that this situation was not good.

The easily gleaned principle found here is that humans need other humans. Man was not created for cloistered independence. The social component of humanity is an essential ingredient that is built into every person. The fact that Eve was created for social connection should provide a clue to what God had in mind for every person, and every human activity, with very few exceptions.

By providing Eve to meet the needs that were created by Adam's aloneness, God instituted marriage. There has been much written about this institution and most of it *does not* apply to this discussion. However, the fact that God instituted two to be the correct number in this institution *is* germane to this discussion. God could have named any other number. However, He instituted two to be the number of individuals in the oldest human institution.

This was the first and is by far the most enduring human partnership. It is bred into humans that two is the proper number. There is something inside every human regardless of race, culture, age, or historical timing that this institution of marriage is sacred. Although there have been many historical and cultural deviations from this standard, they are nevertheless deviations. The proper number in marriage is two.

The primary result of this partnership was the fulfillment of the original command to fill the earth and subdue it. God gave this command to animals and to humankind. Built into His creation is the insatiable desire for procreation. This desire has not diminished even in the face of the evidence that the earth is full of animals and humans. It is as though God never pushed the proverbial off switch for this command. Animals and humans have spent much of their lives in this pursuit.

Redemption from Slavery to Sin

However, due to the seduction of the enemy and the hardness of our hearts, the whole earth became slaves to sin. Every human, since the Fall, has been born with this taint. The sin factor has altered the way humans see things. As a race, humans are bent. We are prone to seek our own way and our own priorities when God has commanded something.

Jesus commented on this slavery and considered it so significant that he called some of those who were "slaves to sin," children of their "father, the devil" (John 8:34, 44). It is interesting that the particular people that Jesus was referring to here were religious people. It is also interesting that these people were perceived as serving the one, true God in the manner of worship that was prescribed by Him. They did not serve God with their hearts, however, and this condemned them. Since they did everything right outwardly, this was hard for anyone, but God, to see.

One of the major themes of the Bible is the redemption from slavery to sin. God, through Christ on the Cross, paid the price to redeem humankind from its slavery to sin. This was the climax to the salvific (salvation) theme in the Bible. When Jesus cried out that it was finished, the fight for this freedom was over. A brief overview of this theme is in order so that this discussion will have a proper foundation.

Section 3 Two by Two Leadership

This is the salvific cause that God began in the Garden of Eden shortly after the Fall of humankind.[39] God not only promised that the fight for freedom would be enjoined and won, but He provided the first provisional remedy in the third recorded chapter of the story of humankind (Gen. 3:15, 21). In the fifteenth verse, He predicted to the woman that her seed would crush the head of the one who tricked and enslaved her.[40] This was the first prophecy concerning Christ.

In the twenty-first verse, God provided animal skins to clothe Adam and Eve's nakedness. There is no record of God creating these skins. In fact, the record of the previous chapters indicated that all physical creation was complete in the first six days of time (Gen. 2:1). For this reason, it is only rational to deduce that God killed at least one animal to obtain these skins. Since this was done in direct response to their sin, it may have been the first sacrifice.

The Old Testament writers carefully chronicled all the main players in the drama of the story of redemption from sin. God sent many ambassadors to men to call them back to Him to the way that they had related in the Garden of Eden. These ambassadors (the prophets) usually only served to drive humankind further away from God.

Moses and Aaron

The reoccurring issues of physical bondage, slavery, or occupation by a foreign power highlighted this drama by providing physical evidence of humankind's spiritual condition. The bondage that the children of Israel experienced in Egypt, for example, was a physical image of the spiritual slavery to sin that controlled their lives. Thus, the work of God to release them from this slavery foreshadowed Christ's work on the Cross. The human leaders in this

---

39 Robert P Lightner, *Sin, the Savior and Salvation: The Theology of Everlasting Life* (Nashville, TN: Thomas Nelson Publishers, 1991), pp. 28-31.

40 Ibid.

first release from bondage were Moses and his brother Aaron. Although Moses was God's messenger to Pharaoh, the actual spokesperson was Aaron (Exodus 4:15-16).

God told Moses what to say, Moses then told Aaron what to tell the pharaoh. It may seem from the conversation between God and Moses that this partnering was a concession that God made to overcome Moses' reluctance to lead. However, God had this partnership in mind before the meeting at the burning bush (Moses' call). He had sent Aaron to find Moses before the meeting ever started (Exodus 4:14). This reuniting of the brothers came after a forty-year hiatus.

The results of this partnership are legendary. For the first and only time in history, a nation of slaves was ejected as a people group from a very powerful nation that had no prior intention of releasing them. She (the nation of Israel) then survived for forty years in a desert until she was ready to enter her new territory. The Children of Israel moved from the place of slavery to the place of freedom as a new nation. This was a type or shadow of what the Lord later did for humankind, and God used a leadership partnership to accomplish this feat.

Once the nation of Israel was established in the land, she (Israel) allowed sin to creep into her ranks. The Lord again allowed bondage to overtake her. This cycle of bondage became a reoccurring theme by the time the Judges arrived (Judges 2:14-23). These leaders were initially successful in deliverance from physical bondage, but they were unsuccessful in enacting any real heart change and turning from sin.

Kings and Advisors

The next phase of leadership was that of the kings. God's original design in this model was for the king to have an advisor to whom he would remain accountable. The first of these royal advisors was Samuel. He not only filled this role, but he was the installer of the king, as well. Sadly, the job of removing the first king

Section 3 Two by Two Leadership

also fell to him. This was precipitated by the arrogant disregard for Samuel's authority on the part of the first king, Saul (I Samuel 15:10-29). This first partnership of its kind failed because King Saul did not recognize that the Lord had not made him the absolute ruler of God's people.

Saul and Samuel were supposed to both be the leaders and rule together. All the successive leaders during this phase in Israel's history either had success or failure mirroring their adherence to this model. If they held to a two-person leadership model, they would have success. When they did not submit to their spiritual counterpart, they failed. An obvious example of one monarch that experienced both success and failure, based on his adherence to this model was Uzziah (II Chronicles 26:1-5; 16-23).

It is obvious to say that David epitomized this phase of Israel's history as her greatest king. It is also safe to say that he had advisors to whom he was accountable. The first of these may have been his supposed chief rival for the throne, Jonathan (I Samuel 20:20-42). They were very good friends, and Jonathan knew that God had given the throne to David (I Samuel 23:17). Jonathan's plan was probably to partner with David as coregents. The Lord intervened, and Jonathan was killed on the same day of his father, King Saul.

David's advisors were many and varied after this. He employed Joab as the commander of his armed forces and other individuals in various leadership capacities. The person who seems to have filled the role of advisor, however, was Nathan the prophet. On at least three occasions, Nathan filled the prophetic shoes and confronted King David (II Samuel 7:17, 12:7 and I Kings 1:24). The most famous one of these was the second when Nathan accused David of horrific crimes. More applicable to this discussion is the last of these confrontations. On this occasion, Nathan anointed the next king, Solomon. This ceremony was engineered

22 Political and Historical Foundations

by David and perhaps was intended as a reminder of Samuel's spiritual authority over the first two regencies.

The period of the Babylonian Captivity and the Post-Exilic period had examples of both successful and unsuccessful partnerships in leadership. On the one side, Nehemiah and Ezra rebuilt not only the physical wall around Jerusalem, but they also reestablished the Law of the Lord as the authoritative rule for the lives of those who lived inside those walls. This partnership was so impactful that the nation of Israel never returned to their besetting sin of idolatry.

On the negative side of this equation, most of the kings who ruled during the ministries of many of the Major and Minor Prophets did not see these prophets as authoritative. The end result was that most of the kings failed in keeping their people from physical bondage. Spiritual bondage to sin was universally accepted as normal. Sin was so rampant that martyring prophets for their messages of impending judgment was considered acceptable.

Before leaving the Old Testament's treatment of this subject, it would be unfortunate not to mention the extensive attention that the Wisdom Literature gave to it. In Ecclesiastes 4:8-12, the teacher presents a vivid picture contrasting the tragedy of being alone and the prosperous joy of having a companion. This is a general statement concerning the damaging effects of being alone, and it mirrors the principle first found in the Garden of Eden that it is not good for man to be alone.

No Hierarchy

God, of course, was undaunted in His plan for the redemption of us, the slaves to sin. He sent Christ to pay the price that was required. He left the rest of the required work of redemption up to His disciples and the church. These, He taught to act like Christ. He also deployed them in training missions and other activities according to the time-honored policy of two-by-two partnership pairings (Matthew 21:1; Mark 6:7, 11:1, 14:13; Luke 10:1, 19:29).

Section 3 Two by Two Leadership

These pairings were not a new idea that Jesus employed for a new dispensation, neither were they experimental attempts at finding a new way of operation. God's principle that it is not good for man to be alone from the Garden of Eden was repeating itself as Jesus laid out the way He intended leadership to function.

If the evidence of the fact that Christ modeled the pairings of leaders was not enough for imitation today, He also provided the rationale behind this policy. All three of the synoptic Gospels record the conversation that He had with His disciples on this subject (Matthew 20:25, Mark 10:42, and Luke 22:25). In these, He compared and contrasted the leadership of the Gentile rulers to that of the new church that was to be created. He contrasted these by taking hierarchy out of the church's leadership equation. In His spiritual family, there were to be no leaders who would "lord it over" the others in the church. To counter any tendencies toward this hierarchy, He institutionalized the policy of sending the disciples "two by two" into ministry settings.

From the context surrounding the sending of these leadership partners into service, it is apparent that the Lord Jesus intended for them to be on an equal footing, authoritatively. One of the disciples was not to be the leader and the other the follower. Rather, they were to share the responsibility and accountability for the success equally. This model made possible the command to not form a hierarchal leadership structure from the outset of the church.

The Purpose is Multiplication

The strategy of the Lord for the spread of the Kingdom of God is multiplication. He is fond of the practice of duplication. On three occasions, Jesus sent His followers away from Him to cause His presence to be expanded in given places. In the first of these campaigns, He sent the twelve disciples out to heal the sick, drive out demons, and preach the Good News of the Kingdom of God. He did this by pairing them up and instructing them as to how they were to conduct themselves and what they were to bring on their journey (Matthew 10, Mark 6:6-13, Luke 9:1-6).

The **second** campaign happened later and was conducted by seventy-two other disciples (Luke 10:1-24). The method was the same as the sending of the twelve. He sent them out "two by two," and they had great success at furthering the message of the Kingdom of God. It is interesting, as a side note, that Jesus commented privately that prophets and kings (the two halves of the Old Testament leadership model) longed to see their day.

The **third** of these campaigns began on the day of Pentecost. Jesus gave specific and different instructions to the disciples concerning this last campaign. *One reason* for this was that Jesus would not be available for the usual debrief about the success of the mission, afterwards. The *second* reason for this was that He would not be available for in person consultation as the mission progressed like He could have been on the first two campaigns. *Third* was that the scope of the mission was to the whole world and not just to the Jews.

The ***last reason*** for this was that this campaign would be very much longer in duration. Because of the tone and timing of His directives concerning this last mission, many have understood this discussion or discourse as having a comforting rather than an instructional motive. Although there is a comforting motive, it is secondary. The real motive to the discussion that the Lord had with the disciples that night was designed to provide final instructions for the last and longest campaign. Let's look now at those directives.

Paraklete

In the "Upper-Room Discourse" Jesus promised that the Holy Spirit would soon come to the disciples (John 14:16). In this discussion, He enumerated the various roles and functions that the Holy Spirit would occupy on behalf of the Godhead.[41] The arrival of the Holy Spirit would only happen after the Son (Jesus) was

---
41 Gary M. Burge, *Interpreting the Gospel of John* (Grand Rapids, MI: Baker Books, 1992), pp. 79-82.

Section 3 Two by Two Leadership

taken away. The Greek word that the Lord used for the Holy Spirit in this passage was *paraklete*.

The word *paraklete* means "one who comes along side to give aide."[42] Jesus utilized this word a number of times in this discussion. However, in this verse, He included the adjective "another" in front of it. This descriptive word in front of the word helper (*paraklete*) means that there will be another helper. There is an obvious question that arises when discussing the modifier "another." Did Christ mean to say that there would be another in *kind* or another in *number*?

If Jesus meant that there would be another in *kind*, then He was probably referring to Himself as the first *paraklete*. It would mean that He was saying that He Himself was the first helper of the disciples and the Holy Spirit would be the next one. In this case, the Holy Spirit would provide another kind of aide to the disciples from the kind of aide that Jesus had provided. There are problems with this interpretation, which will be discussed later.

If, on the other hand, the Lord was meaning that there would be a **second** *paraklete* who was similar in kind to the **first** one, then the obvious question is, who or what was the first *paraklete*? Considering the partnerships from previous campaigns, the answer would have been obvious to the disciples. The disciples would have considered the **first** *paraklete* to be the other disciple in the ministry team. This was the other disciple that they had been assigned to for the first campaign when Jesus sent out the twelve and for the second campaign when He sent out the seventy-two. This was the original buddy system. What Jesus was saying was that the Holy Spirit would become the **third** person in this Two-by-Two system.

---

42 W. E. Vine, *An Expository Dictionary of New Testament Words with their Precise Meanings for English Readers* (Old Tappan, NJ: Revel Company, 1966), singular noun "paraklete."

22 Political and Historical Foundations

If the **first** *paraklete* was to be understood as being Jesus and the word "another" was with respect to different *in kind*, then why did He not say it that way? While it is true that His departure was the signal or prerequisite for the sending of the Holy Spirit, nowhere in the Gospels is Jesus called by this term. In fact, the only reference to Jesus Christ being called the *Paraklete* is in the First Epistle of John. John utilized it in a forensic sense (I John 2:1). In this passage, John said that Jesus is the one who pleads before the Father for forgiveness of the sins of the believer. The word used in this epistle is rightly translated *attorney (Paraklete)*.

Since this is the only reference to Jesus, using this term. It is probably safe to say that He was not calling Himself the first *paraklete* in John's Gospel. The Apostle John probably borrowed this term from Jesus' words in the Gospel to comfort the suffering Christians to whom He was writing his first epistle. It is, however, enough to say that Jesus had someone else in mind as the first *paraklete* when He said "another" *paraklete*.

Since there was no mention in any of the Gospels of the disbanding of the pairs of disciples that were used in the first two campaigns, the reasonable understanding is that they would remain paired for the third and last campaign. If this is true, it is also sensible to understand that the **first** *paraklete* in the minds of the individual disciples was the other half of the pairing. In the case of Peter, he would have understood the **first** *paraklete* as John. Matthew would have understood his **first** *paraklete* as the one that he had been paired with, for example, James. Five pairs would have been immediately cognizant of who the **first** *paraklete* would have been. The exception to this would have been the disciple who had been paired with Judas Iscariot. It is interesting that one of the first things on the agenda for the early church was to replace this missing disciple.

Section 3 Two by Two Leadership

The Early Church

As an apparent continuation of the pairing policy, the early church sent their leaders out in two-by-two pairings, as well. Peter and John were one of these pairs and are found together on several occasions (Acts 3, 4, and 8). Another notable pair was Paul and Barnabas. The exceptions to these are the evangelistic excursions of Phillip (Acts 8) and Peter (Acts 10).

Phillip traveled to Samaria and then to the road from Jerusalem at the behest of the Holy Spirit and was successful in evangelizing many. After his evangelistic efforts began producing fruit in Samaria, the leaders in Jerusalem sent the leadership pair of Peter and John to continue this work. At this point, the Holy Spirit sent Phillip to the road from Jerusalem to Gaza to win the Ethiopian Eunuch to the faith.

In another exception to this pairing policy, Peter had some Spirit-led wanderings that are recorded in the tenth chapter of Acts. These resulted in opening the Gospel to the Gentiles. It is interesting that after the news of this reached the leaders in Jerusalem, they eventually sent Barnabas to the Gentile church in Antioch to investigate the work of God among the Gentiles. After a quick assessment, Barnabas went to find the other half of his eventual leadership pairing, Saul (Paul) (Acts 11:20-30).

The Church Age

To properly follow the progression of this subject after the Biblical record ended, a discussion of the nature of the partnership model is in order. There are two basic (possible) outcomes that are sought when training a person for a leadership role. The particular outcome that is sought determines the nature of the relationship between mentor and disciple.

22 Political and Historical Foundations

Replacement Outcome

First, there is the outcome of a replacement. The nature of the relationship between the mentor and disciple with this outcome in view is that of the change and development of the disciple. There is an urgency that cries for a transformation of the disciple within a certain time limit into something useful to the organization to replace the mentor after he/she is removed for whatever reason.

This is the type of partnership that has dominated the world of leadership both in the church and in the rest of human experience. A gifted leader typically senses his end drawing near, and he seeks to extend the length of time in office by training a successor. This heir to the proverbial throne is groomed to continue the legacy of the previous leader by providing the same kind of leadership as that of the predecessor. This type of partnership in leadership is not only popular in business but also in politics. The reigning monarch generally seeks to train the crowned prince for the difficulties and responsibilities that will challenge him in the future; therefore, the crowned prince is tutored.

The need for discipleship is paramount in Christianity because Christ commanded the making of disciples (Matthew 28:19-20). The reasonable person seeking to obey this directive would begin to make disciples. While the mentor would seek to make these disciples look like Christ, inevitably some of them would tend to look and act like the mentor, especially if the mentor was a particularly charismatic leader. When the end of this leader's life neared, he would begin to feel the need for the ministry to carry on, and so would typically choose the heir apparent.

This heir would then be given access to the inner workings of the original leader's decision-making process, so that the heir would be able to make decisions that mimic those of the original leader. In this way, the legacy of the original leader's ministry would continue. This is how the church has typically followed the

Section 3 Two by Two Leadership

example of Christ to send out leaders two by two. This is the product of making a *replacement* leader.

A good example of this may be found in the succession of the Apostle John. About twenty years before he was to be taken from this earth, John befriended the young Polycarp in Smyrna.[43] The elder influenced the younger, which became a bishop. Polycarp carried this succession on to Iraneous.[44] This sequence and others like it form the Apostolic Succession that the Roman Catholics utilize to legitimatize their Pope's authority.[45] Was this what Jesus had in mind when He sent the disciples out two by two?

Partner Outcome

The second (possible) outcome for a teaming of two leaders is that of a partnership in ministry. Because the outcome of this model is different, the partnership is also dramatically different in several key ways.

First, this type of partnership is different in that it begins not at the end of a leader' ministry, but at the beginning. The idea is not to form a replacement, but a true partner in the ministry. This seems to be what the Lord had in mind when He sent the disciples out in the first place. He was careful to describe the difference to them (Matthew 20:25-28). This description included a clear rejection of the hierarchal model of leadership that is connected to the first (possible) outcome of a *replacement* leader.

The **second** difference between this outcome and that of training a successor is in choosing a potential partner. If the outcome is choosing a successor, then a person who is similar to the original leader is favored. With the outcome of choosing a ministry partner in view, however, the person that would find favor would likely be dissimilar. The reason for this is because the ministry

---

43 Earl E. Cairns, *Christianity Through The Centuries: A History of the Christian Church*, third edition (Grand Rapids, Michigan: Zondervan, , 1954, 1981, 1996) p. 74.
44 Ibid., p. 110.
45 Ibid., p. 117.

would benefit and enlarge with a more robustly diverse leadership team, as opposed to a homogenous team.

The **third** key difference between these outcomes is in training. Training a replacement involves repetition of the *status quo*. What worked with the first leader must be repeated for the replacement. Contrasting this is training for the partnership outcome. This training is concerned with the weaknesses of the other individual in the partnership. The strengths of one individual must correspond to the weaknesses of the other and vice versa. This is required because individual leaders, like all people, have weaknesses. Complementary partners often mitigate these weaknesses.

The **fourth** key difference is in that of the understanding between the partners concerning the division of leadership responsibilities. This naturally follows the previous difference. If one of the individuals in the partnership is weak in a particular area where the other is strong, it is reasonable to allot this responsibility to the stronger of the two. It is conversely reasonable to postulate that the other partner will have natural strength in another areas.

The **fifth** key difference is in the evaluation of the effectiveness of the team. Much can be said about this difference. For this discussion, however, the overall impact on the organization and its corresponding increase in effectiveness is what is in view. The organization must be more effective at meeting the mandates of her charter, for the model to be effective. The exploits and accomplishments of the individual leaders are not on this proverbial table. The individual leader's effectiveness is not in view on this point; the leadership team's effectiveness is.

The **final** key difference is in that of the disbanding of the leadership team. The circumstance that usually surrounds the disbanding of the Replacement outcome is the death or removal of the original leader. This is obviously a sad occurrence, and a period of mourning is in order. After this, the second leader is expected to take over and make any changes that are required to move forward into a new era. The disbanding of the partnership under the Partner

Section 3 Two by Two Leadership

outcome is not as personally dramatic. However, it may produce much more for the Kingdom of God in the long run.

The result of the disbanding of a true partnership is the opportunity for two new partnerships. The best-seen example of this is the disbanding of the Paul / Barnabas leadership team. Paul took Silas as his new partner and Barnabas took John-Mark. They went in two different directions and coincidently trained two more individuals for future partnerships. One of these, John-Mark, went on to partner-up, according to tradition, with the apostle Peter and gained an understanding of the life of Christ that later became the Gospel according to Mark.[46]

Having said all this concerning the outcomes of leadership partners in the church, it is sad to have to report that there is very little evidence of any partnerships in church history that conformed to the requirements of the second outcome. The only one found was that of the Lollards.[47] These people were sent out two by two into the island of England by John Wycliff to read the Word of God in the vernacular of the people. They were some of the forerunners of the Reformation. Their founder, Wycliff, was committed to obeying the Bible in all things and this may be why he obeyed the example of the Lord Jesus in sending leaders out two-by-two. He sent out many of these Lollards. Some have estimated that one in four men in England later claimed this distinction.[48]

---

46 Samuel A. Cartledge, "The Gospel of Mark," *Interpretation, A Journal of Bible and Theology, Studia Biblica, XXIX,* vol. 9, iss. 2. April 1, 1955, p. 188. Accessed Mar. 2024, https://journals.sagepub.com/doi/abs/10.1177/00209643 5500900206#core-collateral-purchase-access

47 Elmer Towns and Vernon Whaley, *Worship through the Ages* (Nashville, TN: B & H Academic, 2012), p. 91.

48 Ibid..

22 Political and Historical Foundations

Chapter Summary

From the above review of the relevant Biblical passages and historical evidence, it is apparent that the need for partnerships in Christian leadership is warranted. It is also a sad commentary on the state of the church that there is only one example of imitating Christ in the Two-by-Two model of Christian leadership found in church history. For this reason, there is very little extra-Biblical information on how this model is to be carried out in modern Christianity. The rest of humankind has not ignored the idea that two are better than one, however, and this data is readily available. This discussion must now turn to this informative resource.

23

Comparing and Contrasting Shared Leadership in Various Fields

To fully appreciate the recent discussion on the matter of shared leadership, it is imperative that proper attention is given to the applicable studies that have been conducted as of late. Although the studies that have the most direct bearing on the subject were conducted in other fields, the findings and conclusions seem to apply to that of the church, as well. After

23 Comparing and Contrasting Shared Leadership

all, the greatest hindrances and benefits to this leadership model were found in the intangibles of human nature, and these are very similar in every field.

Shared Leadership in Nursing

Although others have made more headway and deeper observations in shared leadership, none have had a greater impact as of late than Sandra Jackson. Working in her chosen field of nurse management, she has defined the parameters of how shared leadership is to be evaluated into the near future. She provided an article, outlining her study findings entitled, "A Qualitative Evaluation of Shared Leadership Barriers, Drivers and Recommendations." In this article, she provided the field of shared leadership with four descriptive characteristics known as constructs. These four descriptive characteristics have already served as guidelines in forming and understanding this newly inaugurated leadership model.

Although she credited Tim Porter-O'Grady for the bulk of her insight, the organization of the four characteristics were plainly Jackson's contributions.[49] By setting these four constructs, she ushered the idea of shared leadership from vague obscurity to delineated study. These four useful attributes have been added to the discussion, and it is forever on the proverbial shared leadership map. The model of shared leadership owes her a debt of gratitude.

Four Constructs

The **first** of these four constructs is a **decentralized organizational structure**.[50] Rather than upholding the hierarchal leadership model where all the decisions are made at the top of an organization, the shared leadership model accommodates and, in fact, requires decisions be made at the level of the staff who will

---

49 Sandra Jackson, "A Qualitative Evaluation of Shared Leadership Barriers, Drivers and Recommendations" *Journal of Health Organization and Management,* Volume 14, No. 3/4, Aug. 1, 2000, pp. 166-178. Accessed Feb. 2024. https://www.emerald.com/insight/content/doi/10.1108/02689230010359174/full/html
50 Jackson, "Shared Leadership," p. 167.

carry out the decisions. This makes sense if the goal of an organization is efficiency and effectiveness. The old leadership model focused accolades and/or blame on the the leadership at the top of the hierarchy based on the success or failure of their decisions. The new model is not as concerned with these as it is with the productivity of the teams.

The **second** of these constructs is **a balance of *autonomy, guidance, collaboration, and accountability*.**[51] This construct is the heart and structure of the shared leadership model. The fact that these four must be in balance is of crucial importance. If one of these moves too far off center and becomes the focus of the organization, then the organization suffers. All of these must progress and grow with the others in mind for this balance to be maintained. The idea behind this construct is not unlike the checks and balances that exist in the government of the United States. The four parts of this construct must govern each other, so to speak, in order to facilitate shared leadership.

Autonomy is the understanding that each member of the team has a place that he or she must occupy. Each member must work to fulfill his or her respective role so that the organization may complete its mission. In a professional setting like nursing, the implications and application of this part are obvious. Not only are there specialists who may be called upon to perform certain tasks, but also the specialists themselves are further ranked according to competencies and experience. When all members of a team find fulfillment in the respective roles for which they are best employed, a level of autonomy of the individual begins to emerge.

Guidance, according to the old models, is the direction that is given to the subordinates from above in the chain of command in order to cause something to happen in a correct manner. The old adage, "The boss is always right," is what is in play here. However, when the shared leadership model is employed, the question is

---

51 Jackson, "Shared Leadership."

23 Comparing and Contrasting Shared Leadership

rightly asked, "What if he is wrong?" Under the shared leadership model, the person who has the correct information is the person who has the task of informing the others in the team. The idea is that no one is right simply because they hold some office or occupy some role. Truth is what is valued, not political wrangling. This plays to every member's strengths. It also minimizes the weakness of any one member.

Collaboration is the idea that the team is always more important than individuals. The "lone wolf" is not only seen as out of date, but also counterproductive. The objection to collaboration that is usually raised at this point is something about how the need for someone to stand-alone against rampant foolishness outweighs the need for collaborative teamwork. This objection presupposes two thoughts: *First*, that the great majority of professionals in the workplace are little more than mindless lemmings following each other over the proverbial cliff of some unnamed catastrophe. *Second*, that the person with this objection sees the catastrophe and its cause. Both presuppositions are probably stretching the truth.

Collaboration is found when individuals in teams begin to emphasize the strengths of their fellows to meet needs. Further, it is when teams with particular strengths emphasize and rely on the particular strengths of *other* teams to meet goals. Furthermore, it is when organizations with strengths emphasize the strengths of other organizations to effect real change in society. President Truman best encapsulated all that is required for collaboration to occur: "It is amazing what you can accomplish if you do not care who gets the credit."[52]

Accountability is often seen as the reality check of any organization. Any product is seen as wonderful until the inspector's unbiased observation points out flaws. Accountability does not allow the inspector to be fired in favor of a blemished product. If this does

---
52 Harry S. Truman, "Harry S. Truman Quotes," Good Reads Inc. Accessed June 2024, http://www.goodreads.com/author/quotes/203941.Harry_S_Truman.

Section 3 Two by Two Leadership

occur, the client or consumer will reprimand that organization by finding another organization that will deliver a quality product.

As professionals, it is not only important to follow the previous three parts of this construct, but also to do whatever needs to be done, and do it correctly. Accountability is the right and responsibility of any team member to say that the product is not up to quality standards. When leadership is truly shared, this is not seen as an oddity at all. Rather, as fellow leaders, the team members eagerly adopt this and the other three parts of this construct.

The **third construct** is an **environment of excellence**.[53] The idea here is that every member of the organization sees his or her individual position as vital to the success of the mission and performs at his or her best in every task. There was once a junior executive in training that was placed under the tutelage of a run-of-the-mill housekeeper. The executive was given the task of cleaning a hospital bed for placement of a patient. After the executive cleaned the bed, the housekeeper got under the bed and really cleaned it, showing the executive the level of excellence that was expected in that organization. This executive was marked by this experience for the rest of his tenure at that organization.

This third construct further shows itself when the organization constantly strives for **continuous improvement**. Every organization has either actual or potential rivals. If the incumbent organization in a market niche is not continually seeking to improve the product, it can rest assured that another organization is working to figure out how to produce something better, or at least a more attractive alternative. If only to ward off the threat of being replaced, every organization should give attention to this segment of this construct. While it is easy to see that this construct is vital for an organization to even survive, all too often, old leadership models focus on maintaining the *status quo*.

One area that needs another look is the make-up of the leadership model. In the nursing profession, this look has happened,

---

53 Jackson, "Shared Leadership."

23 Comparing and Contrasting Shared Leadership

and the results are very encouraging. There are new ways of looking at the structures of organizations. This shows that the shared leadership model not only has merit, but also may be transferable to other fields. When it comes to excellence and continuous improvement, the shared leadership model is a largely untapped resource.

The **fourth** construct is a **shared vision** within the organization.[54] Here Jackson began down the familiar path of the classical leadership model. This includes the four parts of *vision, communication, positioning and the ill-defined fourth one* that includes the integrity of the leader. However, she stopped at the first part. Rather than continuing with *communication, positioning and the personal character of the leader*, she simply let the shared vision carry the organization into action and success. This is a triumph for the shared leadership model in that it bypasses the other three parts of the classical model and streamlines their functions into the daily work schedules of every individual in the organization.

Rather than planning an annual event for the top leader to announce and sell the vision to the organization, this construct requires communication to be constantly buzzing concerning how to implement the shared vision. This vision is rooted in the shared values of the members of the organization. Not only is this communication being done concurrently with the necessary work, but the need to "sell" the vision is also removed from the model. Since everyone shares the vision in the first place, the question is not whether individuals accept it, but rather how they may fit into it with other leaders.

The need for the third classical part of the leadership model (positioning) is also trumped in that people find their own place in the organization, based on their strengths, and not in someone else's *opinion* of their strengths. The shared leadership team comes into its own in this area of vision development. The team will ferret

---
54 Jackson, "Shared Leadership."

Section 3 Two by Two Leadership

out the overly ambitious individuals that may think themselves more capable than they are. The team also will advance the individual that is strong in any area.

In addition to these four constructs, Jackson's work also uncovered the axiomatic statement that epitomizes shared leadership at its core with respect to management and staff: "The staff are accountable for the work of the organization, and management is accountable to support the staff and the environment so that the work can be completed effectively and efficiently."[55] It is interesting that this mimics the apostle Paul's directives in Ephesians 4:11-14. The leaders of the church are to equip the saints for the work of ministry.

If these contributions were not enough, Jackson also provided *barriers, drivers, and recommendations* with respect to her model of shared leadership.[56] Although this section of her findings was self-evident and redundant, the principles bear repeating. **The barriers** were as follows: the fact that the whole process was *very costly in time spent*, the *resistant attitudes* of the staff, and the "*mental models*" that were *set to old leadership styles*. These three *barriers* were easily overcome compared to the fourth and *final barrier*. The process, with its plethora of *meetings,* was seen by most of the staff as a *waste of time,* as it took them away from their perceived role as caregivers for their patients.

The drivers included strong support and commitment from senior levels of leadership in the organization. Strong lines of communication and dialogue were other requisite drivers. An organizational structure which supports the shared leadership model was also included. A clear evaluative process for refinement finished the list of drivers for shared leadership to thrive in an organization.

The recommendations that Jackson presented were in line with the need to remove the above-mentioned barriers and

---

55 Jackson, "Shared Leadership," p. 167.
56 Ibid., pp. 168-169.

23 Comparing and Contrasting Shared Leadership

promote the above-mentioned drivers.[57] At this point in her paper she encapsulated the four constructs into one word each. These were *accountability, partnership, equity, and ownership*. These abbreviated buzzwords have been utilized by other studies, which will be discussed later in this book. They represent the mental models that will be helpful for a broader application into other fields, like Christian ministry.

While this study was very helpful to set the foundation for implementation and evaluation of the shared leadership model, most of it was not easily conducive to a broader application for other fields besides nurse management. There is a need for a more direct study of the benefits and implementation of the shared leadership model in a partnership leadership setting. This more direct study will be discussed in the next chapter.

Two-Getherness

The next study that has a place in this discussion took the idea of shared leadership in nurse management from the theoretical to the practical. Utilizing an existing shared leadership situation in Sweden, researchers conducted a series of interviews with a pair of nurse managers that shared a common intensive care unit under their charge. These interviews spanned the initial three-year period that the two managers worked together in this role. The insights that were gained were not only enlightening, but they were also helpful in further refinement of the shared leadership model for other fields. The article produced was entitled, "Supporting 'Two-Getherness': Assumptions for Nurse Managers Working in a Shared Leadership Model."[58]

One term that came from the two participants in the study was *Two-Getherness*. "This term was coined by the participants to

---

[57] Jackson, "Shared Leadership."
[58] Kristina Rosengren and Terese Bondas. "Supporting 'Two-Getherness': Assumption for Nurse Managers Working in a Shared Leadership Model." *Intensive and Critical Care Nursing*, v. 26, issue 5, Oct. 2010, pp. 288-295. Accessed Mar. 2024. https://www.sciencedirect.com/science/article/abs/pii/S0964339710000674.

Section 3 Two by Two Leadership

mean a connection that minimizes their individual weakness while maximizing their individual strengths in a trustful relationship that is able to share responsibilities and tasks equally."[59] This definition is loaded with content and bears further examination. The synergistic attributes about minimizing weaknesses while maximizing the strengths of the partners is easily transferable to other fields and has implications for Christian ministry. The requisite trust is included because a partnership of this type demands it. The fact that responsibilities and tasks are included reminds the readers that there must be a product or service that is the outcome of the shared leadership situation.

Two-Getherness is more than just a catchy term that may become the new buzzword with respect to this subject. It is the very heart of how shared leadership is possible and why it is necessary. For example, if the two individuals in the leadership partnership happen to possess the same particular strength, this strength is thusly duplicated. In this case, one of the strengths of one of the partners is redundant. Usually, the one that possesses this strength to a lesser degree is relegated to the background in the relationship if this strength is important in the leadership context. A rivalry is therefore set-up between the two individuals in the shared leadership situation, and this is not conducive to Two-Getherness.

Conversely, if only one individual in the leadership pair possesses a skillset with the aforementioned strength then the other individual in the pair is free to explore his or her unique strengths. Ideally, these strengths will complement and augment the other individual's strengths. Perhaps this strength will mitigate any inherent weakness in the first individual's skill-set. For this reason, pairing individuals with similarities may be a barrier to success of the shared leadership model.

One of the other important findings of this study in the nuts and bolts of shared leadership was that of the new roles that the

---

59 Rosengren and Bondas, "Two-Getherness."

23 Comparing and Contrasting Shared Leadership

managers found themselves playing in the intensive care unit. Because the decision-making process evolved into a collaborative effort between the two of them, it was natural for them to enlarge the circle of trust in this area to include the nursing staff. For this reason, the two managers found that their role changed from controlling to teaching and mentoring.[60] They realized that many of the decisions that they had previously made on a regular basis were no longer presented to them because their staff felt empowered to make these decisions without them.

The other major finding in this study is reflective of a finding in other studies on this subject. The two managers individually expressed a newfound confidence that came from the trusting relationship that they shared with their counterpart.[61] It was as though they stopped worrying about their individual inadequacies and weaknesses because they knew that their partner could cover that part of the leadership responsibilities. Instead, they focused their individual energy into making their strengths benefit the intensive care unit. This confidence led to all kinds of empowered enablement among the staff, which then led to a much-improved unit.

This study has a great deal of promise concerning a more direct application to Christian ministry because ministry is like caregiving in many ways. The idea of Two-Getherness goes far in expressing the kind of requisite relationship that is needed for two individual leaders to work together effectively. However, there are a few glaring realities that must be acknowledged. *First*, nursing and Christian ministry are not the same field. For this reason, those in the latter may not accept the success found in a study on the former. *Second*, Christian ministry works with volunteers to care for others who do not always see the need for their services. Conversely, the nursing profession works with paid staff to care for those who acutely feel the need for their services.

---

60 Ibid. p. 289.
61 Ibid., p. 291.

Section 3 Two by Two Leadership

Shared Leadership in Christian Ministry

The next study was general in nature. It explored the morale of the individuals who happen to be in a shared leadership model organization already. These organizations were Christian ministries in the United States. The study was focused on the negative relationships between the shared leadership model and role overload, role conflict, role ambiguity, and job stress. The study also positively looked at the relationship between the shared leadership model and job satisfaction in the team members. The working description of the shared leadership model was a "concept that has grown from the realization that leadership can be effectively shared or distributed among members of a group or team."[62]

The study asked and answered a question with respect to the relationships between the shared leadership model in practice in Christian ministry and the positive or negative factors. The findings surprised the investigators, especially with respect to the negative factors. The investigators had assumed that the ever-present role ambiguity in the shared leadership model would naturally lead to higher rates of role overload and role conflict, leading to higher overall job stress. This expectation, however, did not materialize into reality overall. On the contrary, the exact opposite was found to be true. The more the shared leadership model was in place, the lower were the levels of job stress.[63]

Another question that was asked and answered in this study was concerning the type of organizational culture that would incubate the shared leadership model most effectively. The study found that an organizational culture that was based on a traditional, hierarchal leadership model would be resistant to embracing the newer leadership model. Conversely, if an organization was based on

---

[62] Michael Shane Wood and Dail Fields, "Exploring the Impact of Shared Leadership on Management Team Member Job Outcomes." *Baltic Journal of Management,* vol. 2, iss.3 (2007), pp. 251-272. Accessed Mar. 2024. https://www.proquest.com/docview/208674357/75EC6B4410B64EB9PQ/1?sourcetype=Scholarly%20Journals

[63] Ibid., pp. 4-5.

23 Comparing and Contrasting Shared Leadership

team operation, the shared leadership model seemed to not have any trouble thriving.[64]

Although the authors of this study did utilize Sandra Jackson's general constructs in no apparent organizational order with respect to recognizing shared leadership in action, they did not directly quote her. They emphasized empowerment and accountability as two firm foundations for this model. This was a good study for this book because it focused on the demographic for this project, that of ministry professionals. However, the idea of shared leadership in the minds of the investigators of this study was merely seen as a division of labor along blurred lines of responsibility. While it is useful in that it showed the general benefits of an organization starting in the direction of shared leadership, it did not address the specifics of partnerships in ministry.

The next study concerned itself with the need for diversity in the top management teams (TMT) of large churches. Eighty-two churches from a single denomination were the focus of this study. The main thought behind the study was that modern "churches are less neighborhood institutions than collections of people who are similar in some way."[65] This being the case, the idea was that prospective members would gravitate to and attach to a leader in the church who was somewhat like them in some way. The more ways that the TMT members connected with any given individual, the higher the probability was that this individual would consider that church his or her home. For this reason, diversity in the age, socioeconomic status, racial and cultural heritage or style among the members of the TMT may attract and assimilate more new members.[66]

The results were interesting in that they did support the idea that the overall attendance in churches with a diverse TMT

---

64 Ibid.
65 Clay D. Perkins and Dail Fields. "Top Management Team Diversity and Performance of Christian Churches." *Nonprofit and Voluntary Sector Quarterly,* vol. 39, iss. 5 (July 31, 2009). p. 827. Accessed Mar. 2024. https://journals.sagepub.com/doi/abs/10.1177/0899764009340230.
66 Ibid., p. 833.

Section 3 Two by Two Leadership

membership tended to be above that of non-diverse TMT membership. However, there was a surprise finding that indicated that the overall monetary revenue in these diversely managed churches was lower than the non-diverse.[67] The implications of these findings are clear. The churches that would impact their communities greatly with the Gospel must allow for a diverse team of leaders, but they may have a hard time doing it with less money.

The last study for this review was concerned with the question of whether there was just cause to study pastoral effectiveness in the first place.[68] One hundred one senior pastoral leaders were interviewed. These interviews focused on the feelings of these leaders concerning their pastoral effectiveness. Three areas of measurement included **Golden rule leadership, intentional leadership, and trusting God.**[69] These three epitomes of the pastoral role were looked at as being the benchmarks of pastoral effectiveness.

The first of these, **Golden rule leadership**, was simply what the name implied. The leader was encouraged to regularly ask and answer the question: "Have I led others as I would have them lead me?" This question spoke to the integrity and character of the leader as he or she conducted the affairs of the church. Although this area of study was largely subjective in nature, it fit with the study overall.

Intentional leadership was concerned with the classical functions of leadership in that it formulated vision, communicated vision, and positioned people into roles that help carry out the vision. This part of the study was more objective than the rest of the study in that it looked at specific markers, rather than feelings.

The third measure was the idea behind **trusting God** in the pastor's personal sphere. Beyond numbers and staff, the pastor

---

67 Perkins and Fields. "Top Management Team Diversity," p. 836.
68 Robert B McKenna and Katrina Eckard. "Evaluating Pastoral Effectiveness: To Measure or Not to Measure." *Pastoral Psychology*, vol. 58, iss. 3 (June, 2009), pp. 303-313. Accessed Mar. 2024. https://link.springer.com/article/10.1007/s11089-008-0191-5
69 Ibid., p. 306.

23 Comparing and Contrasting Shared Leadership

needed to find his or her comfort in the belief that God Himself was in control of the situations that were encountered. This third measure spoke to the pastor's effectiveness at being a follower of Christ in general.

While this study was limited in that it was largely based on the perceptions of the pastors who were being studied, it was helpful in that it showed that evaluation and examination has its place. The all-too-common practice of placing pastors on the proverbial pedestal needed a second look. The conclusion of the study was that pastoral effectiveness does merit further study and that the examination itself could provide benefits for the Kingdom.

There needs to be a discussion at this point concerning the four classic views on church government. These have been identified as Episcopal, Presbyterian, Single-Elder Congregational and Multiple-Elder Congregational.[70]

The Episcopal system of church government is characterized by a hierarchal organization that is ruled by a central figure or bishop. The Presbyterian system of church government employs a central committee that governs multiple local churches.

The last two systems of church government employ a more democratic form in which the people in the local congregations largely determine who leads them. The Two-by-Two model of church leadership seems to fit with the second of these, Multiple-Elder Congregational. The acceptance of other leaders in an organization is foundational to the Two-by-Two model. There is little room for those who would be rivals in the other three church leadership views. While the Two-by-Two model does fit within this view, the specifics of the model set it apart effectively. There will be a more thorough discussion of this in chapter 25, page 203.

---

[70] Steven Cowan, *Who Runs the Church?: Four Views on Church Government* (Grand Rapids, MI: Zondervan, 2004) pp. 12-15.

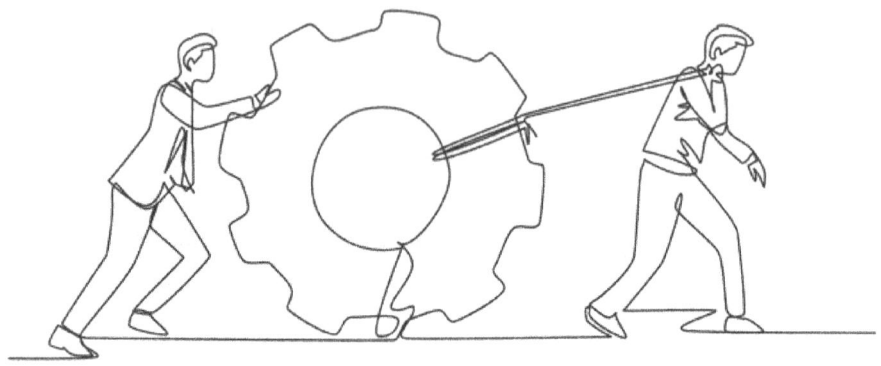

24

The Church Case Study

The second part of the research for this discussion in this section focused on a new church in a city on the Atlantic seaboard. This ministry was founded by two pastors and was led by these same two pastors. These two leaders were committed to the idea that partnership leadership was preferable to solo leadership. In fact, the human instigator of this church (Phil) would not move to the city in question and start the church until the other one (Bill) agreed to do it with him. It would be an understatement to say that they were fully committed to the Two-by-Two model of leadership.

The research began many months before this book was written. A prolonged period of observation was needed for the researcher (me) to not only determine that partnerships in Christian leadership were needed, but also to observe the interaction of the particular personalities of the leaders. This part of the research was very informative, indeed.

Although they were in their early thirties, the pastors were fully educated and experienced minsters of the Gospel before they began planting the church. The idea began in the mind and heart of Phil as he began to feel the leading of the Lord to plant a church about ten years earlier. Years later, after attending a yearlong church planting course/internship in the southern part of the country, he felt the leading of the Lord to relocate his family to the east coast city. He also felt that the leadership team needed to include Bill as a real partner in this plant.

So Phil called Bill on the phone and began the process of forming their partnership. Although this was the first of several calls that were needed for the partnership to be fully formed, there was intentionality to Phil's actions that showed that he placed a high value on the partnership.

Phil is a quiet person at his core. His serious demeanor and patient contemplation added much to the beginnings of planting the church. This is juxtaposed to his role as the primary preacher and teacher on Sunday mornings. He is thoughtful and introspective as he interacts with those under his spiritual care. He is a gifted teacher and speaker, and administration is obviously in his arsenal of gifts.

Bill is a people person. He is all about grace and mercy when he interacts with those under his spiritual care. There is a welcoming air about him as he works with those who are outside the body of Christ, as well. Bill is an energetic extrovert who generally interacts very well with all those he contacts.

The church plant had been doing well until a few months before this researcher arrived and discovered the partnership. The researcher gleaned insight as he conducted interviews and field observations not only on the two persons mentioned, but also on the ministry that they were leading. This was a turbulent time for this church, not because of the leadership, but because the Lord was preparing the leaders and the church for significant growth.

Section 3 Two by Two Leadership

Both Phil and Bill had begun to feel discontent with the church plant. The numbers had plateaued and the general feeling among the partners (their name for members) was that there needed to be something more. Phil and Bill earnestly sought the Lord's direction during this time and felt that they needed to wait for Him to act on their behalf.

Soon after this researcher discovered their partnership, Phil and Bill renewed their commitment to making disciples as their first and only goal in the ministry. This was a move away from their innate desire as church planters for numbers. They seemed to shift gears at that time and stopped worrying about quantity in their ministry while they focused on the quality of the disciples that were being produced. This shift drew several seminary-trained, experienced leaders to their ranks.

One of the **first** observations I made was that Phil was very good at preaching the doctrine of grace. This seemed to be somewhat of a contradiction to his personality which seemed to be about doing things right. His personality type would argue that there must be an exacting standard, but his sermons emphasized the need to find this standard fulfilled in Christ. By the way, his sermons on grace were very well received.

Meanwhile, Bill would preach on the responsibility of Christians to obey the commandments of Christ. This was very well received, perhaps because this teaching contrasted with his personality, which was all about grace and mercy. This contrast between Bill and Phil's personalities and their life messages was very significant. It was as though they were transforming into their partner while they occupied the pulpit. It would have been beneficial for this researcher to have been the proverbial fly on the wall during their early conversations concerning their respective roles and messages.

This brings up the **second** observation. Wherever one of the partners had a weakness, the other had an inherent strength. They called their weaknesses "dislikes" and their strengths "likes." In their meetings, when a task would surface that one of them needed to complete, one would say that he did not "like" to do it. This became code for the understanding of the other one that he really was not very good at doing that task. Very often, the other one did "like" to do it, which meant that he was quite good at it. For this reason, the partner that was the best at the task did it and often did so with confidence and excellence. Once they became comfortable delegating to each other in this way, the partnership began to gel in earnest.

A **third** observation was that both Phil and Bill operated in a very confident manner both publicly and privately. This may have been due to their submission to one another's authority in their lives and ministries. For whatever reason, this confidence was infectious and attractive. They drew more than a handful of Christian leaders to their ranks as fellow partners (members).

One of the indicators of effective Christian leadership is the ability to make needed changes in the ministry. About five years into the church plant, they acutely began to feel the need for a church building. Phil and Bill wisely presented this burden for a church building to some of the other leaders that had joined the plant. They submitted to the will of this group and moved into a building that was ideal for large parties. The net gain from this move was astounding. Not only was there a renewed emphasis on discipleship, but also a further influx of experienced leaders augmented the ranks of those who were making disciples.

To utilize the resources that the Lord had obviously given them, they began to employ these experienced leaders into the life and leadership of the church. These experienced leaders had many different views on how a church should be governed and were not shy about voicing these differing opinions. The fact that the two pastors were significantly younger and less experienced in the ministry than these leaders never became an issue. On the contrary, their youth and inexperience was seen positively as tools for

Section 3 Two by Two Leadership

reaching the new generation for Christ. The fact was that there was such an air of confidence and authority emanating from the two of them that they were rarely questioned concerning the validity of their new ways and innovations.

This reoccurring idea that the elevated confidence level of the co-leader in a shared leadership model situation easily refers to the Sweden Intensive Care nurse management case study in chapter 23. The idea of "Two-Getherness"[71] is admittedly subjective and open for misinterpretation, but it does provide the individual leader in a partnership with some valuable tools. One of these tools is confidence.[72] It may be the case that these two young pastors could stand up under the pressure of conformity to the *status quo* that came from the older leaders because of their "Two-Getherness."

Another benefit, derived from "Two-Getherness" is the mitigation of the individual leader's weaknesses because of the corresponding strength in his or her partner.[73] The converse of this is true in the ministry of the other individual in the leadership pair. Both of their weaknesses are diminished in direct correspondence to their openness and submission in that area of their lives to their partner. Their partner is supernaturally endowed with strength that augments this weakness. The honesty level between these two nurse managers was sufficient to bring about the "Two-Getherness."

Bill and Phil decided to train the leaders that were joining the church in the methods that were valuable to them and the mind-set behind those methods. They utilized the book *The Trellis and the Vine* in this pursuit.[74] This book turned many of the established norms in church polity on their proverbial heads. "Trellis work," the term for those activities in ministry that do not directly make disciples, is valued much less than in other models of ministry. "Vine work," conversely, is the term for activities in ministry

---

71 Rosengren and Bondas, "Two-Getherness."
72 Ibid., p. 291.
73 Ibid.
74 Colin Marshall and Tony Payne, *The Trellis and the Vine. The Ministry Mind Shift that Changes Everything*, Second edition, Australia: Matthias Media, 2021.

24 The Church Case Study

that directly cause disciples of Christ to be made. This is given top priority and most of the resources of the ministry need to be used in these activities.

The two pastors asked the experienced leaders to read this book and provide feedback. If any of these leaders came back with negative pushback on this book, their leadership would be valued less in the church plant. Once one of these newly assimilated leaders embraced the notion that discipleship was the highest valued activity in that church, they began to be placed in increasingly more strategic positions. Although it was never stated outright, the book became a training and operational manual for the polity of this church plant.

Although allowing a book besides the Bible to operate in this capacity is dangerous, the pastors were wise in implementing it in two ways. *First*, they never said that it filled this role outright. They simply began to follow the steps that were enumerated in it. Because all the leaders that had been placed in significant positions had given their approval, this unofficial policy was never challenged.

Second, they introduced the various components espoused in the book slowly and with Biblical authority. For example, Phil, who usually filled the pulpit on Sunday mornings, began to downplay the importance of the Sunday morning sermon in favor of the people living sermons for their friends and families. This was in an apparent effort to conform to the eighth chapter in the book.[75] This chapter is all about how the sermon is vital, but not enough to make viable disciples.

To utilize the leaders that were beginning to join the church, Phil and Bill began two new small groups and instituted another level of leadership in the existing groups. Following some counsel, they decided to allow a place among their leadership model for women. Initially their position was restricted to hospitality, but it

---

75 Marshall and Payne, *Trellis*, pp. 93-108.

Section 3 Two by Two Leadership

finally extended to that of mission leader teams as well. The ranks of official leaders grew from 8 to 16 with this move alone. The women partners worked well together and successfully expanded their mission and outreach programs.

Despite this, there were still more than a few un-utilized leaders that considered this plant their church home. For this reason, Bill began to charge the existing leaders with the duty and privilege of discovering new leaders and developing their potential. The idea that leaders need to be identified and promoted from within the ranks of the existing church body comes right out of chapter ten in the above-mentioned book.[76] In this chapter, the authors show that the Biblical source for leaders is the church. That's where the leaders came from and were developed in the first place. This led to another doubling of the small groups over the next twelve months.

It is important to underscore the point that this *Get Out Of the Boat* book is not meant to be shining a negative light against the church. It has opened the discussion concerning the need for another look at the idea of innovation in the church of Jesus Christ. Although chapter 26 gives suggested steps for implementing the Two by Two model, it is not meant to be a step-by-step manual for a new kind of church and should not be expected to fill this role. The Bible is the only legitimate source for such an endeavor. Having said this, the fact is that this book is one of the ever-increasing numbers of books that are calling for a serious second look at how the Western culture does church. This look needs to start with Biblical directives and normative practices. It further needs to incorporate these into a current culture in order to reach that culture. Let's look deeper now at how that can be accomplished.

---

76 Marshall and Payne, *Trellis*, pp. 127-142.

25

The Two-By-Two Leadership Model for Christian Leadership

This project has thus far shown that there are serious problems facing the leadership of the modern church. The leadership model that has been in force since the fourth century is at the heart of the problem. This model is known as the Constantinian model. The leadership that it promotes is the solo, hierarchal model and is hard to see in the New Testament.

Section 3 Two by Two Leadership

The solution to this problem may be found in returning to the example of Christ in forming leadership partnerships. This chapter is offered as a possible reference for implementation of the Two-by-Two model for Christian leadership.

The discussion thus far about leadership partnerships in the Christian church has yielded several insights. *First*, there is indeed a problem with the current leadership model. This model includes the idea that solo leadership is not only acceptable, but also that it is the ideal situation. *Second* the review of applicable literature and research studies held that there is a crisis in the leadership of the modern church and that team leadership is preferable to solo leadership. *Third*, the applicable Biblical references showed that solo leadership was not the model that the Lord promoted.

The Two-by-Two Model

The solo leader in the local church is a monstrosity. Its base of support may come from the felt need of many in leadership for control. This need has no place in Christian circles. This felt need is altogether misplaced. The need for the leader to feel that he or she is in control is out of bounds in the Christian experience. The fact is that the Lord Jesus Christ Himself claimed to be the One in charge, and He does not share this charge. He declared that He would build His church, and the very gates of hell would not prevail against it (Matthew 16:18b). The Lord is very much in control of His church via the agent of the Holy Spirit.

Having said this, it would be a misstep to ban leadership in the church. The fact is that the Lord set up leaders in His church and charged them with leadership tasks. The problem is that God's human leaders have always had a propensity for overstepping their bounds. In the absence of the physical presence of the Lord, spiritual leaders tend to do things that do not please Him. Aaron, for example, made an idol when he did not know what else to do (Exodus 32:1-9). The result of this action caused the destruction of the original tablets of stone and endangered the first Exodus.

25 The Two by Two Model for Christians

In addition to the literary and Biblical evidence provided in this project, there is research that has taken place during its entirety. A survey showed that those who are now in leadership partnerships are very satisfied, at least among the research participants. They have a high degree of confidence and satisfaction as they face the issues in their various ministries. There was also the case study of the new church planted by the Phil and Bill partnership that was conducted to determine some "best practices" with respect to the Two-by-Two model.

There is ample evidence that the model of leadership that includes solo leaders in the church of Jesus Christ is debunked. Not only this, but the idea that the true model that needs to be recaptured is that of leadership pairs or partnerships. Another look at the Biblical record is in order now to determine what kind of individuals work best with others in leadership capacities.

Paul and Barnabas

It is established that the Biblical standard operating procedure for leading is Two-by-Two teams. Is it a stretch to try to further discern what the specific pairs are like? It is interesting that the New Testament pairs who are named are Peter and John, and Paul and Barnabas. It is not far fetched to see that Peter and Paul were similar and that John and Barnabas were similar.

Peter and Paul were clearly leaders, and they tended to take on the role of spokesperson for the groups to which they were attached. They both also wrote or dictated multiple books in the New Testament. John and Barnabas, on the other hand, were all about people. Their ministries showed this quite well. John was also a writer, but his books are not theological in nature. Rather, they have an application orientation. He and Barnabas were known to cause people to become all that the Lord had for them to be. For the sake of clarity, the first of these personality categories will be labeled *Paul* and the second type of leaders will be labeled *Barnabas*.

Section 3 Two by Two Leadership

It is noteworthy that the Lord (via the Holy Spirit) was the one who paired Saul (Paul) and Barnabas. One of the only mentions of the Holy Spirit instructing the church directly concerns the subject of this partnership (Acts 13:2). On this occasion, the Holy Spirit instructed the leaders of the church at Antioch to set apart Saul (Paul) and Barnabas for a work that He had for them to do. This became the First Missionary Journey, which is recorded in the book of Acts.

Paul was a leader that was all about truth and the letter. He had his terminal degree and was well on his way to becoming one of the top religious leaders in his sect when the Lord confronted him and changed his tune. However, the Lord did not change Paul's basic bent with respect to his gifts and personality. The Lord wanted to utilize his hard-charging, type-A personality for the Kingdom. The control on Paul's temperament came in the form of the subjective internal leading of the Holy Spirit and a co-leader named Barnabas.

When all the facts of the story are told, it was Barnabas, under the directive of the Holy Spirit, that went to Tarsus and found Saul (Paul) to bring him to Antioch and put him to work (Acts 9:27; 11:25). It has been suggested that Saul was a bit discouraged at that time in his life. The believers in Jerusalem had just previously shunned him because they were suspicious of him due to his violent past. They had extended to him the right hand of fellowship but did not fully trust him. So, he went home for an undisclosed period.

Barnabas was thusly nicknamed as the son of encouragement. His real name was Joseph, and he was a people-person. He was all about finding the people that needed edification and lifting them up to service for the Lord. He was known for acts of generosity that became the catalyst for many others' generosity in the early days of the church in Jerusalem. The fact that he was the one that went to a possibly discouraged Saul to put him back in service

25 The Two by Two Model for Christians

makes perfect sense. He did not stop with Paul in his ability to make a broken disciple useful.

The facts that surround the break-up of the first missionary team find Barnabas nursing John-Mark back to leadership health. As I pointed out before, this John-Mark became the guy who was credited with writing the Gospel of Mark as a compilation of the stories about Jesus, which were recounted by Peter.

As the book of Acts informed us, it was in the middle of the First Missionary Journey when John-Mark left the team and went home. If he was a leader cut from the same mold as Paul, the reason for this defection was obvious. Paul and John-Mark clashed. Anytime two strong personalities are forced to live with each other, they butt heads. Later, the soothing Barnabas came back to John-Mark and showed him how it was unacceptable for him to leave. Paul still did not trust this young upstart who was perhaps nothing but trouble before he left. The result was two new teams. Nonetheless, in the end, Paul did see the usefulness of John-Mark (II Timothy 4:11).

There was another person who was in the company of Paul who was so much like him that it is possible that they clashed. A careful reading of the narrative in the book of Acts concerning Paul's missionary journeys will reveal some "we" passages and many more "they" passages. Doctor Luke was the human author of the book of Acts, and he inserted himself into the story when he was present. It is interesting that he was only present during the first part of the Second Missionary Journey. He apparently stayed in Philippi during most of this trip. It is pure speculation to try to ascertain why, but it is likely that Luke was another strong personality. The potential for needless personality conflict was very high. The point is, "Pauls" tend to clash with each other, so do not put them on a Two-by-Two team together.

After recognizing that "Pauls" tend to clash, it would appear that the only personality type fit for Christian leadership would be

Section 3 Two by Two Leadership

"Barnabases." However, this is not the way that the Lord has done it in the past, and it will not work in the future. Two "Barnabases," if paired together, would love each other into lethargy. They would be so polite and affirming that they would get nothing else done. They need to be attached to their respective "Pauls" to be prodded into service. They need a "Paul" to keep them on track and going somewhere. Without "Pauls," "Barnabases" flounder. They look like great leaders, but they do not go anywhere, and they tend to lead the rest of the church there as well.

This idea is firmly grounded in the previously established principle that the shared leadership team needs to be populated by pairs with complementary strengths. Bill and Phil could find comfort and confidence in the fact that the other in their partnership was strong where they were weak. This led not to competition, but to greater confidence and ultimately growth. This is also largely what was intended by the term *Two-Getherness* that was coined in the Sweden Intensive Care nurse management shared leadership study.[77]

It is interesting to note that the particular strength of a leader may be an accurate indicator of an inherent corresponding weakness. It has been said that every leader in history was plagued with classic, glaring faults.[78] The strategy to mitigate these faults is to pair a leader with a fellow that he or she trusts in the ministry to be his or her *leader*. This person must exhibit strengths that will offset the first leader's weakness.

Some "Pauls" have so alienated the modern church with their hard-charging fanaticism that they are often marginalized as proverbially too heavenly minded for any earthly worth. Their visions and plans are seen as too grandiose and far-fetched. What they need is a real Barnabas to come alongside and lead with them. The plans that they have are often from the Lord and are the right plans. However, without a "Barnabas" to "sell" these plans, many

---

77 Rosengren and Bondas, "Two-Getherness."
78 Howard Hendricks, lectures on leadership, Dallas Theological Seminary, 1994.

will never be adopted. What the church of Jesus Christ needs, to get back on track, is a right understanding that no one is an island, least of all leaders. "Pauls" need to know that they are less effective without their "Barnabases." "Barnabases" need to know that although they might look good as leaders, they do not have the whole picture, and their ministry is incomplete without their respective "Pauls."

There is another obvious application to this simple Two-by-Two pairing that is needed. Any future leadership teams who are commissioned need to bear these differences in mind. It is foolish to continue to ignore the need for Two-by-Two leadership or to ignore the facts concerning "Pauls" and "Barnabases." Once a person (leader) knows who he or she is, this person can begin to look for their respective partner. Leadership developers need to be looking for these pairs and to be pairing them together, as well.

Identifying Leaders

There seems to be some questions with respect to the initial identification of leaders. After all, since everyone cannot lead and there are only limited resources, who should receive leadership training? How do these leaders surface? What qualities should be seen in individuals as leadership attributes that are the base elements of potential leaders?

Born or Made?

One of the first questions that must be asked and answered on the subject of leadership development is where they come from; are they born or made? In secular circles, this is a question that polarizes those who have knowledge of the subject. The person who would argue that leaders are born into leadership would point to the plethora of evidence that some great leaders begin leading from early childhood. These leaders seem to come out of the womb with a scepter in their little hands. These people exhibit the classic, outward signs of leadership from very young ages and begin

Section 3 Two by Two Leadership

leading in earnest in their early teens. Some of the greatest political and military leaders from history may be seen in this light.

Alexander the Great, Cesar Augustus, and others were great leaders from their teens and would be good arguments for the "leaders are born" camp. However, biased, leader-worshipping followers wrote the records on these, so the histories of these men may be suspect. There may have been not a few legends on how these men became leaders to bolster their greatness. Leaders who fall into this category also had the very best tutors (Alexander had Aristotle) and this is a very good argument for the "leaders are made" camp.

All this banter goes out the proverbial window when considering leaders in the Christian camp, however, because all Christian leaders are both born and made. Christians are born in Christ and made into His image. Christian leaders are to have already been through these early phases before they begin training for leadership.

In Small Groups

One of the most effective environments for the identifying and training of leaders is the small group. A great deal of real spiritual growth happens in one-on-one mentoring or in small groups. There is no substitute for this intensive nursery.

The most important goal for the small group leadership team is that of making disciples. The second goal is to multiply groups. Developing the next generation of leaders does this. However, the question remains, how is the future leader identified? The answer lies in natural group dynamics.

After the group starts up, the leadership team (partnership) must immediately begin the process of identifying future leaders. There are two types of Biblical leaders. We must specifically identify who is the "Paul" and who is the "Barnabas." The clue to which is which may be found in their natural strengths and corresponding weaknesses.

The second-generation untrained leader will exhibit certain characteristics inherent to his bent. For example, the raw "Paul" will question everything, while the future "Barnabas" will seem very caring and sensitive. Most small group leaders see untrained "Pauls" as problems. Not a few have secretly hoped that they would quit coming to the group. Conversely, the "Barnabas" of the next generation will be so into helping others that it is often difficult for the group leaders to draw them out and help them with their own growth.

Development and Training of Leaders

Once they have been identified, future leaders may be placed in their own small group for leadership training. This group will consist of four to ten individuals led by a facilitating partnership of two who have experience at equipping leaders. At the outset, all participants in this new **leadership training group** would be informed that they are being groomed for leadership. The fact that they will someday make their own groups is part and parcel of their future as Christian leaders. No one will be given a group; they will build their own.

The group that these new leaders will build will consist of the various people in their spheres that are not already in a Christian small group. Most of these individuals will first need to be introduced to the Savior. They will need to be taught to hear the Lord's Voice for themselves and to begin to obey Him. For this reason, the new leaders themselves will need to become firm in their own faith so that they will be able to train others in knowing and following the Voice of the Lord.

One of the many checks and balances that must accompany these kinds of groups to avoid deformity will be the requisite deployment of the new leaders in pairs. One of these leaders will naturally check his or her partner when the other begins to lean

Section 3 Two by Two Leadership

toward error. The error may take many forms, not the least of which may be pride. A confrontational discussion can be kept in confidence so that the group will not need to suffer. Many of the errors that leaders currently fall into would be averted if the leader had someone to talk to that was on their perceived level. For this reason alone, the need to send leaders out in leadership pairs is obvious even to the casual observer.

Based on the needs of the church and the new leader, the new leader will officially plan to stay in the leadership training group for six to eighteen months. However, this group often becomes a haven for most new leaders, and is never disbanded until the members of it move away or graduate to their final home.

These weekly support/leadership training meetings are the key to keeping the leadership on track. We have found that when leaders meet like this for support, accountability, and prayer with their peers, they keep making disciples for a long time. Under the current solo leadership church model, pastors are largely confined to solitude. They live very lonely lives as they do their very best. As we have seen, the Two-by-Two leadership is Biblical and far superior to the solo-model.

Leaders need to have other leaders to lean on, regularly and often. We have found that if we make this meeting weekly and compulsory, new leaders soon begin to see the benefit. At any job, there is benefit in a cohort. Even if the workers only see each other once a week, they are able to debrief in a non-threatening atmosphere. By the way, no one is the boss at these leadership training meetings. They are led by the two partner facilitators, but the Holy Spirit sets the agenda.

Without these three elements of support, accountability, and prayer in their weeks, many Christian leaders secretly quit the ministry once a week. Most hear the Voice of the Lord encouraging them, and they do not tell anyone about their resignations. In the

25 The Two by Two Model for Christians

Two by Two model, other leaders supplement this encouragement to persevere.

This support meeting is a non-threatening atmosphere for pastors. Support can take many forms. Sometimes it is listening to a leader vent about whatever might be troubling him or her that week. The individual pastor finds a colleague (usually the same one each week) who can share in his hurts and joys; who can give and pray so that they both can feel like someone cares.

As a pastor for a very long time, I can attest that this is what is missing and causing many pastors to quit most Monday mornings. As mentioned, for the pastors who only have the Lord to comfort them, they find the courage in the Holy Spirit by Monday afternoon to carry on, barely. Is this the way we want our leaders to operate? In the Two by Two model, when leaders meet once a week for support, they receive reassurance, determination, and confidence to keep on persevering in their ministry of making disciples.

Leadership Training Curriculum

The curriculum that is utilized for leadership training must fit the facilitation partnership and those who are being developed as leaders. It must also be transferable. A transferable curriculum must not only be able to be used by the new leaders when making disciple makers of their own, but it must also be available when the time comes for the new disciples to do so. One that has a track record for being successful on both levels is the *Design for Discipleship* by the Navigators.[79] This is a very helpful resource for this purpose.

Although this Bible study workbook series covers many topics that concern the Christian walk and discipleship, much of the series is devoted to propagating the four basic disciplines: the Word of God, prayer, witnessing, and fellowship. These four disciplines

---

79 Chuck Broughton, *Design for Discipleship*, 6 vols. (Colorado Springs, CO: Navpress, 1973).

make up the foundation that causes the followers of Christ to walk correctly. The leaders in training must incorporate these activities into their lives so that the four disciplines become second nature. These four disciplines are the skills that they will need to model for future followers of Christ. Special attention needs to be paid, at this juncture, to the motivation of the leaders in training.

The mentor needs to be especially attentive as to why the new leaders are keeping these disciplines. The sense that a person may read their Bible or pray simply to put the proverbial check in the box is not acceptable. They need to keep the disciplines so as to please Christ. Not seeing Him as a taskmaster that demands certain activities, but as a friend that wants to spend time with them. The former motivation will lead to legalism; the latter to a walk with Christ that will survive until the end.

Once the new leaders are well into the curriculum, they must be deployed into service so that the cycle may continue. This may be begun very early in their training so that they may use and retain what they are learning. The timing for full deployment is ill-defined because it is different for every individual. A leader is no longer a follower (at least when he or she is leading); however, followers of Christ never stop following Christ. This is an ever-present tension that should never fade in the mind of the leader over the course of his or her life. With this in mind, one of the indicators that a person is ready to be given Christian leadership responsibilities is when he or she begins to listen to and obey the voice of the Lord.

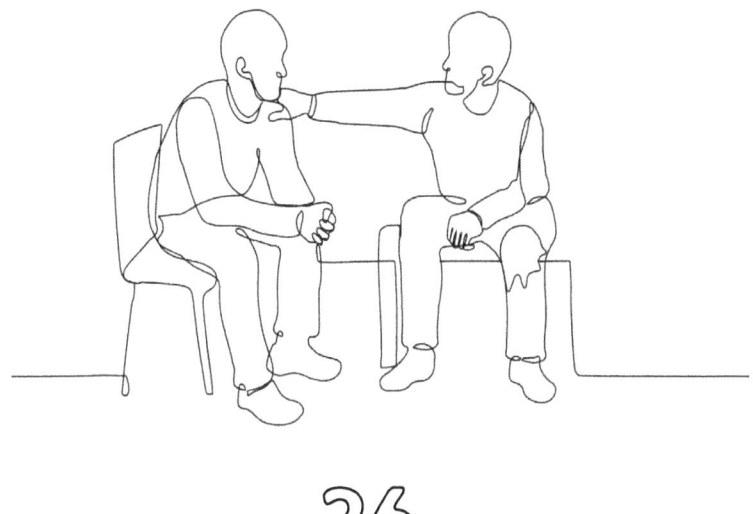

26

Fourteen Steps for Transitioning a Ministry to the Two By Two Leadership Model

Before I launch into the nuts-and-bolts of how to implement the Two-By-Two model into an already existing ministry of another flavor, I need to insert a disclaimer. The previous chapters of this third section of this book (Two-By-Two Leadership) were initially written as part of my dissertation in pursuit of my Doctor of Ministry degree. My mentor required me to add this last chapter as an application for the implementation of the new model for church polity. What he did not know was that I

Section 3 Two by Two Leadership

was then in the process of becoming de-churched. I felt that I needed to become de-churched to reach de-churched people. The ministries that I have helped to pioneer since then have not only reached de-churched people, but also some from other demographics, as well.

I know now that there is no one-size-fits-all model for the modern church that would hope to reach the world for Christ. Also, the de-churched demographic in the United States is still only about fifteen percent of the population.[80] In my zeal, I may have caused some Christian brothers and sisters in leadership to start to feel that I have devalued their walks and practices. I apologize for this. I know that it will take all of us to reach the nearly 8 billion souls that are breathing air today. It will also take the real source of our power (the Holy Spirit) to reach them. He wants us to come to Him on a daily basis for renewed enthusiasm and instructions. If this book has helped you to see this, then please forgive any non-intentioned slights that my words may have caused.

It is very important at the beginning of any activity in Christian ministry to pray. This not only causes our Creator and Sustainer to help in the activity, but it also causes the individual that prays to enter a proper understanding of his or her role. The correct understanding of the role of the Christian leader is that of a responding facilitator. Jesus said, *"Without me, ye can do nothing"* (John 15:5b KJV). While prayer is officially the fifth step, it is very important to bathe this whole process in prayer.

The Fourteen Steps

Step one is the understanding that **Jesus Christ is the chief** designer and builder of His church (Matthew 16:18). It would behoove any who would aide Him in church leadership to remember this. With this in mind, it is only fitting that those who lead do so His way. One of the keys to this is to remember that He never

---

[80] Anderson, Neil T.. *The Bondage Breaker*. Eugene, OR: Harvest House Publishers, 2000.

26 Fourteen Steps for Transitioning to Two by Two

sent His followers into any ministry situation except two by two. If a Christian leader is found in any other situation, he should amend this situation.

Step two is the recognition that the leader **cannot do the ministry alone.** Howard Hendricks said, "Never go anywhere without somebody."[81] There needs to be another leader that joins the solo leader in ministry. Doing ministry alone is not the way Christ intended it.

The **third step** is for the leader to **recognize what kind of leader he or she is**. This is difficult and it takes some time. If the leader is focused on rules and requirements, then there is an easy case to be made that this leader may be a "Paul" type. Conversely, if the leader is almost entirely concerned with the growth of individuals, then this leader may be a "Barnabas" type. The problem is that people do not tend to fall strictly into one of these two parameters. There are shades of the two types of leaderships in most leaders. The requirement in this step is for the leader to determine his or her primary, natural bent. This bent may be seen in interactions with other leaders. If the leader has worked well with people who are like Paul, then this leader may be a Barnabas type. The same is true in the converse. A natural Paul will tend to not work well with other Paul types.

Step four is for the leader to **recognize possible partners** that are in or around his or her ministry. If the potential partner is untrained as a leader, he or she will be easier to identify. Untrained Paul types tend to question every answer. In small groups, this person is the proverbial thorn in the leader's side. People who lead like Barnabas tend to reach out and comfort others in small groups, even before they have been trained in leadership. This makes them easier to identify as Barnabas types.

---

81 Howard Hendricks, "Lectures on leadership," Dallas Theological Seminary, 1994.

Section 3 Two by Two Leadership

Because of the important upcoming decisions to be made, **step five** is a **season of prayer.** The leader must pray for courage and wisdom. The next few steps may shape his or her effectiveness in ministry and should be clearly in subjection to the specific direction of the Holy Spirit. Prayer is key to gaining this insight. Prayer also shows that the leader is dependent upon the Lord. Prayer is a significant barometer of the faith level of the leader. It is also an indicator of the object of the leader's faith.

Step six is the **proclamation** of this model **in public** settings. Sermons should begin with the Biblical mandate that it is not good for man to be alone. It would not be wrong to spend a good deal of time preaching on this topic from the pulpit. People need to understand that there may have been some failings in previous church leadership models. People also need to understand that Jesus provided His way of leadership.

Step seven is for the leader to **approach God's choice for the co-leader.** The leader should **humbly ask** for assistance from this person. The leader must remember that this person will tend to not be in perfect subjection to the first leader's values. If the first leader is a person who leads like Paul then the co-leader will be a person who leads like Barnabas. The key to this step is respect. If the first leader truly respects the ministry of the co-leader, then it will work. If not, it will not.

The **eighth step** revolves around **small group ministry.** If there is not a small group element to the existent ministry, one must be started. The reason for this is that leaders are developed in small group settings. The eighth step is to begin the process of transferring the Two-by-Two model to the next generation. People who lead like Paul and people who lead like Barnabas must be identified. They must be taught their specific strengths and weaknesses. They then will be able to see how having a partner with complementary strengths is important.

26 Fourteen Steps for Transitioning to Two by Two

Step nine is **pairing up** the two types into tentative partnerships. People who lead like Paul need to be paired with people who lead like Barnabas. If Frank is of the first type, he should be paired with Joe of the second type. It is important that both Frank and Joe understand their roles in this partnership. This cannot be overstated. If Frank or Joe thinks they are solely in charge of the ministry, or solely subservient in this partnership, it will not work. It should be noted that the two types do have differing strengths and should take charge in certain circumstances. People who lead like Paul should lead in Bible studies and discussions about responsibility. People who lead like Barnabas, conversely, should take over when individual needs are expressed in the small group. They also should lead discussions about practical applications that arise from Bible studies.

There are two elements to the model that must be understood at this point. *First*, the two leaders should consider their partner, their leader. The first leader should consider the second leader to be his leader and vice versa. This will provide a confidence level that will rarely be shaken. *Second*, the two of them should begin to champion each other's messages. The leaders who lead like Paul might begin to preach grace, which is the natural message of the Barnabas types. Conversely, the Barnabas types may publicly articulate the message of responsibility, which usually comes from Paul types.

The **tenth step** is **deployment**. Beginning with small assignments, the leadership pairs should begin to spread their proverbial wings and lead in small group settings. This may be accomplished in a variety of ways. One very good practice is for the facilitating partnership to be in constant contact with individuals who are willing to be a part of an outreach team. This team is to be tasked with starting a new group in order to accommodate the context of the new leaders having a place to lead. The idea is for a team of individuals to be available to be the "core" for new team formation.

Section 3 Two by Two Leadership

When the new leaders experience success in small things, they should be given larger responsibilities. Not every leadership pair will be able to lead in every circumstance. Some leaders are not destined to lead large numbers of people. However, early failure at leading large numbers of people does not necessarily disqualify leaders for this task.

Step eleven is **monitoring and evaluating** the teams that have been deployed. Jesus did this in His first two campaigns. He sent His disciples out in Two-by-Two pairs, and then brought them back for times of debriefing and refreshment. During these times of debriefing, He acknowledged their excitement over their perceived success, and spoke of His unseen insights into their real success (Luke 10:18-19). It is important to be positive if there is any success at all. This is not a model which should be tried and discarded quickly. This is the model that Jesus employed.

Step twelve is to **make needed changes**. Even utilizing the Two-by-Two model, some individuals will not be partnered correctly. Leaders are not foolproof. There should always be the realization that mistakes can be made. The fact that two people are not successful together does not diminish the need for solo leaders to have a partner. The original Paul and Barnabas actually parted ways in anger. Remember that in Acts 15 Paul took Silas and went on the second missionary journey. Barnabas took John-Mark and went on his own missionary journey. Although they did reconcile (Colossians 4:10), the fact is that these two were angry enough that they did not work together again. The wonderful fallout from this was that one team became two.

Step thirteen is to realize that there is a need for many more echelons of leaders in fulfilling the great commission. If the leaders of subsequent generations begin to train leaders, this is very good. Paul mentioned **the need for four generations of leaders** in this verse: *And the [instructions] which you have heard from me along with many witnesses, transmit and entrust [as a deposit] to reliable*

26 Fourteen Steps for Transitioning to Two by Two

and faithful men who will be competent and qualified to teach others also. (II Timothy 2:2 AMPC). Paul was the first level, Timothy was the second, *reliable and faithful men* were the third level, and *others* were the fourth level.

This is a good goal with respect to the subject of discipleship effectiveness. If someone who has never even met the original leader brings people to Christ, the effectiveness of the discipleship effort is no longer contingent upon the first leader's effectiveness. This discipleship effort will continue well beyond the ministry of the first leader.

The **last step** revolves around the **original leader leaving** that ministry. It is natural for a strong leader to feel the need to replace his or herself. Obviously, someone needs to step into the leadership role that will be vacated. However, if the co-leader was firmly established as leader, then there will not be a felt vacuum in the leadership structure of that ministry. There will be time for the new co-leader to be identified and to replace the original leader according to the direction of the Holy Spirit. It is acceptable for the original leader to leave with a junior of the opposite leadership type. According to the previously mentioned schism between Paul and Barnabas, both leaders left Antioch with a co-leader.

These fourteen steps are not set in proverbial granite and may be amended to fit the individual needs of the ministry. The ideas behind these steps do need to be implemented. However, the order and essence of the steps is open for broad application according to the specific leading of the Holy Spirit. This list of steps is not to be seen as exhaustive either. There will probably be other steps that are necessary as the model begins to be employed. The goal is for the Two-by-Two model to be taken seriously. Every ministry needs to examine itself with respect to how it is to be fully engaged.

Section 3 Two by Two Leadership

Summary

It has been shown that partnerships in leadership in the church are to be preferred over solo leadership models. Further, it has been shown that the specific personalities that are best paired are those who have been labeled "Pauls" with those who have been labeled "Barnabases." When properly understood, the idea that some leaders are "Pauls" and others are "Barnabases" will be a great help in furthering the identification, development, and deployment of future leaders.

There is a plethora of innovations that are being fostered as ways to reach the new generation for the cause of Christ.[82] These are being implemented by many church leaders in the hope of finding the magic ingredient that will help them make a dent in the ever-increasing gap between the general population and church growth. This gap is real and may not go away because of the usual cultural norms and expectations from previous generations. The best way to reach this generation for Christ is to revisit the directives of Scripture and amend the church of today accordingly. This book includes a call for the leaders of the church to do this. In doing so, they may legitimize and nurture the efforts of the next generation of church leaders to find and follow the Lord's directives for reaching the subsequent generation. If they fail to do this, they may squelch vine work for the next generation.

The Lord Jesus Christ urged His followers to pray the Lord of the harvest for more laborers (Matthew 9:36-38). This was just after He saw the multitudes and had compassion on them because they were like sheep without a shepherd. The church today may need to throw aside her prideful ways and come back to Biblical directives. Her leaders may need to come back to the example and commands of Christ and lead together to reach this lost and dying world for Christ. There is little time for the status quo when the masses are still like sheep without a shepherd.

---

82 Elmer Towns, et. al., *11 Innovations in the Local Church*.....

26 Fourteen Steps for Transitioning to Two by Two

BIBLIOGRAPHY

Anderson, Neil T.. *The Bondage Breaker.* Eugene, OR: Harvest House Publishers, 2000.

Barna, George. *Growing True Disciples.* Colorado Springs, CO: Water Brook Press, 2001.

_____. *The Power of Team Leadership: Achieving Success Through Shared Responsibility.* Colorado Springs, CO: Water Brook Press, a division of Random House, Inc. 2001.

Bennis, Warren. *Essential Bennis.* Hoboken, NJ: Jossey-Bass, 2009.

_____. *On Becoming a Leader.* Reading, MA: Addison-Wesley Publishing Company, 1994.

Bennis, W. and Burt Nanus. *Leaders: Strategies for Taking Charge.* New York, NY: Harper and Row, 1985.

Blackaby, Henry and Richard Blackaby. *Spiritual Leadership: Moving People on to God's Agenda.* Nashville, TN: B&H Publishing Group, 2001.

Broughton, Chuck. *Design for Discipleship.* 6 vols. Colorado Springs, CO: Navpress, 1973.

Burge, Gary M. *Interpreting the Gospel of John.* Grand Rapids, MI: Baker Books, 1992.

Cairns, Earle E. *Christianity through the Centuries: A History of the Christian Church.* third edition, Grand Rapids, MI: Zondervan, 1954, 1981, 1996.

Carson, D. A. *The Gospel According to John.* Grand Rapids, MI: William B. Eerdmans Publishing Company, 1991.

Cartledge, Samuel A. "The Gospel of Mark." *Studia Biblica* (1955), 188. Accessed Mar. 2024. https://journals.sagepub.com/doi/abs/10.1177/002096435500900206

Cawthorne, Jon E. "Leading from the Middle of the Organization: An Examination of Shared leadership in Academic Libraries." *The Journal of Academic Librarianship* Vol. 36 (March, 2010). Accessed Mar. 2024. https://www.sciencedirect.com/science/article/abs/pii/S0099133310000078.

Cole, Neil. *Organic Leadership: Leading Naturally Right Where You Are.* Grand Rapids MI: Baker Books, 2009.

Collins, Jim. *Good to Great: Why Some Companies Make the Leap… and Others Don't.* New York, NY: Harper Collins, 2001.

Covey, Stephen R. *The 8th Habit: From Effectiveness to Greatness.* New York, NY: Free Press, 2004.

Bibliography

———. *The 7 Habits of Highly Effective People: Powerful Lessons in Personal Change.* New York, NY: Simon & Schuster, 2004.

Cowan, Steven, *Who Runs the Church?: Four Views on Church Government.* Grand Rapids, MI: Zondervan, 2004.

Anderson, Neil T.. *The Bondage Breaker.* Eugene, OR: Harvest House Publishers, 2000.

De Roest, Henk. "The Precarious Church: Developing Congregations in an Individualized Society." *Ecclesiology* 4 (2008). Accessed Mar. 2024. https://www.researchgate.net/publication/233639284_The_Precarious_Church_Developing_Congregations_in_an_Individualized_Society

Driscoll, Mark. *Confessions of a Reformissional Reverend.* Grand Rapids, MI: Zondervan, 2006.

Duin, Julia. "Just in: Latest Church Growth Statistics." *The Washington Times*, February 12, 2010. Accessed Mar. 2024. https://www.washingtontimes.com/blog/belief-blog/2010/feb/12/latest-church-growth-stats-in/

Duvall, Scott and Daniel Hays. *Grasping God's Word: A Hands-On Approach to Reading, Interpreting, and Applying the Bible.* 2nd ed. Grand Rapids, MI: Zondervan, 2005.

Fee, D. G. and D. K. Stuart. *How to Read the Bible for All Its Worth: A Guide to Understanding the Bible.* 2nd ed. Grand Rapids, MI: Zondervan, 1993.

Foster, Richard. *The Celebration of Discipline: The Path to Spiritual Growth.* New York, NY: HarperCollins, 1998.

Fox, John. *Book of Martyrs*. John Dat, 1563.

Fuller, Jim. "Statistics in the Ministry." Pastoral Care Inc. Accessed Mar. 2024. http://www.pastoralcareinc.com/statistics/

Gomez, Pamela Wesley. "Life's Lessons of a Lay Leader." *Anglican Theological Review*, vol. 92, issue 1(2010). Accessed Mar. 2024. https://www.proquest.com/docview/215262590/6E31C59EDE7E-452APQ/1?sourcetype=Scholarly%20Journals

Hendricks, GPN Dr. Howard - "Living By the Book" video series, Dallas Theological Seminary, YouTube. Accessed Mar. 2024. https://www.youtube.com/watch?v=S55huHC_0_k&list=PLHVLAsJuPfmUeA6eOavI0NheF8Ra0sLu2

Hesselgrave, David J. *Planting Churches Cross-Culturally: North America and Beyond.* 2nd ed. Grand Rapids, MI: Baker Publishing Group, 2000.

Iorg, Jeff. *The Painful Side of Leadership: Moving Forward Even When It Hurts.* Nashville, TN: B&H Publishing Group, 2009.

Jackson, Sandra. "A Quantitative Evaluation of Shared Leadership Barriers, Drivers and Recommendations." *Journal of Health Organization and Management* Vol. 14, No. 3/4, Aug. 1, 2000. pp. 166-178. Accessed Feb. 2024: https://www.emerald.com/insight/content/doi/10.1108/02689230010359174/full/html

Jessup, Harlan R. "New Roles in Team Leadership". *Training and Development Journal,* 44 (Nov. 1990). Accessed Mar. 2024. https://eric.ed.gov/?id=EJ416086

Jordan, Robert *The Dragon Reborn (Wheel of Time #3).* New York, NY: Tor Books, 1991.

Kent, Homer A. Jr. *Jerusalem to Rome: Studies in the Book of Acts.* Grand Rapids, MI: Baker Book House, 1972.

Kerr, J. R. "Open Source Activists." *Leadership Journal* 30.3 (Summer 2009). Accessed Mar. 2024. http://www.christianitytoday.com/le/2009/summer/opensourceactivists.html.

Klein, William, Craig Blomberg, and Robert Hubbard. *Introduction to Biblical Interpretation.* Nashville, TN: Thomas Nelson, Inc., 2004.

Kouzes, James and Barry Z. Posner, ed., *Christian Reflections on the Leadership Challenge*, San Francisco, CA: Jossey-Bass Publishers, 2004.

Krejcir, Richard J. "What is Going on with the Pastors in America?" *Schaeffer Institute of Church Leadership Development,* 2007(research from 1989 to 2006 with 2016 update). Accessed Mar. 2024. http://www.churchleadership.org/apps/articles/default.asp?articleid=42347&columnid=4545

Lightner, Robert P. *Sin, the Savior and Salvation: The Theology of Everlasting Life.* Nashville, TN: Thomas Nelson Publishers, 1991.

LaSor, William S., David A. Hubbard, and Frederic W. Bush. *Old Testament Survey: The Message, Form, and Background of the Old Testament.* 2nd ed. Grand Rapids, MI: Eerdmans Publishing Co., 1996

Lausanne Committee for World Evangelization. "The Local Church in Mission: Becoming A Missional Congregation in the Twenty-First Century Global Context and the Opportunities Offered Through Tentmaking Ministry." (Lausanne Occasional Paper No.39).

MacDonald, William. *True Discipleship.* Kansas City, KS: Walterick Publishers, 1975.

Bibliography

Malphurs, Aubrey. *A New Kind of Church: Understanding Models of Ministry for the 21st Century.* Grand Rapids, MI: Baker Books, 2007.

_____. *Strategic Planning: A 21st-Century Model For Church And Ministry Leaders,* Grand Rapids, MI: Baker Books, 1999, 2005, 2013.

_____. "The State of the American Church: Plateaued or Declining," *The Malphurs Group,* Sept. 5, 2014. Accessed Jun. 2024. https://malphursgroup.com/state-of-the-american-church-plateaued-declining/

Marshall, Colin and Tony Payne. *The Trellis and the Vine: The Ministry Mind-Shift That Changes Everything,* second edition, Kingsford NSW, Australia: Matthias Media, 2021.

McGavran, Donald A. *How Churches Grow.* London, England: World Dominion, 1959.

_____. *Understanding Church Growth.* 2nd rev. ed. Edited by C. Peter Wagner. Grand Rapids, MI: Eerdmans Publishing Company, 1990.

McGavran, D. A., and Win Arn. *How to Grow a Church.* Ventura, CA: Regal, 1973.

McGavran, D. and George C. Hunter, III. *Church Growth: Strategies That Work.* Nashville, TN: Abingdon, 1980.

McKenna, Robert B. and Katrina Eckard. "Evaluating Pastoral Effectiveness: To Measure or Not to Measure." *Pastoral Psychology,* vol. 58, iss. 3 (June, 2009), pp. 303-313. Accessed Mar. 2024. https://link.springer.com/article/10.1007/s11089-008-0191-5.

Mitchell, Michael R. *Leading, Teaching, and Making Disciples.* Bloomington, IN: Cross Books, 2010.

Neck, Christopher P. and Charles C. Manz. "Team Leadership in Practice." *Thrust for Educational Leadership.* vol. 28, no. 2, pp. 26-29 (Nov-Dec 1998). Accessed Mar. 2024. https://eric.ed.gov/?q=%22Team+Leadership+in+Practice%22+Thrust+for+Educational+Leadership%2C+Nov-Dec+1998

Nelton, Sharon. "Team Playing is on the Rise." *Nation's Business,* vol. 84, issue 6 (June 1996). Accessed Mar. 2024. https://www.proquest.com/docview/199817251/CD9F492F09A14B91PQ/1?sourcetype=Magazines.

Perkins, D. Clay and Dail Fields. "Top Management Team Diversity and Performance of Christian Churches." *Nonprofit and Voluntary Sector Quarterly,* vol. 39, issue 5 (July 31, 2009). Accessed Mar. 2024. https://journals.sagepub.com/doi/abs/10.1177/0899764009340230

Poirier, Alfred. *The Peace Making Pastor: A Biblical Guide to Resolving Church Conflict.* Grand Rapids, MI: Baker Books, 2006.

Porter-O'Grady, Tim. "Whole Systems Shared Governance: Creating the Seamless Organization." *Nursing Economic$* 12 (July 1, 1994). Accessed Mar. 2024. https://europepmc.org/article/MED/8945273.

Putman, David. *Breaking the Discipleship Code: Becoming a Missional Follower of Jesus.* Nashville, TN: B &H Publishing Group, 2008.

Rainer, Thom S. and Eric Geiger. *Simple Church: Returning to God's Process for Making Disciples.* Nashville, TN: Broadman & Holman, 2006.

Reid, Alvin L. *Radically Unchurched: Who They Are and How to Reach Them.* Grand Rapids, MI: Kregel Publications, 2002.

Rosengren, Kristina and Terese Bondas. "Supporting 'Two-Getherness': Assumption for Nurse Managers Working in a Shared Leadership Model." *Intensive and Critical Care Nursing* vol. 26, issue 5, Oct. 2010, pp. 288-295. Accessed Mar. 2024. https://www.sciencedirect.com/science/article/abs/pii/S0964339710000674.

Sande, Ken. *The Peacemaker: A Biblical Guide to Resolving Personal Conflict*, Second Edition. Grand Rapids, MI: Baker Books, 1997.

Schwarz, Christian A. *Natural Church Development: A Guide to Eight Essential Qualities of Healthy Churches.* St. Charles, IL: Church Smart Resources, 1996.

Stott, John R. W. *The Message of the Sermon on the Mount (Matthew 5-7): Christian Counter-Culture.* Downers Grove, IL: Inter-Varsity, 1985,

Tertullian, Quintus Septimus Florens Apologeticus, L. 13, translation by Alex. Souter with introduction by John E B Mayor, Cambridge University Press, 1917.

Thompson, Jr., Oscar W. *Concentric Circles of Concern: Seven Stages for Making Disciples.* Nashville, TN: Broadman & Holman Publishers, 1999.

Towns, E. L. and Ed Stetzer. *Perimeters of Light: Biblical Boundaries for the Emerging Church.* Chicago, IL: Moody Publishers, 2004.

Towns, Elmer, Ed Stetzer, and Warren Bird. *11 Innovations in the Local Church: How Today's Leaders Can Learn, Discern and Move into the Future.* Ventura, CA: Regal Books, 2007.

Towns, Elmer and Vernon Whaley. *Worship through the Ages.* Nashville, TN: B & H Academic, 2012.

Bibliography

Towns, Elmer and Dr. Yonggi Cho, *Praying the Lord's Prayer for Spiritual Breakthrough: Daily Praying the Lord's Prayer As A Pathway Into His Presence.* Bloomington, MN: Bethany House Publishers, 1997.

Truman, Harry S., "Harry S. Truman Quotes," Good Reads Inc. Accessed June 2024, http://www.goodreads.com/author/quotes/203941.Harry_S_Truman.

Tummillo, Michael. "Surviving an American Church Split." (Mar. 13, 2006) Accessed Mar. 2024. https://www.faithwriters.com/article-details.php?id=41071.

Twigg, Nicholas W. and Bomi Kang. "The effect of leadership, perceived support, idealism, and self esteem on burnout." *Journal of Behavioral Studies in Business* (April 2011). Accessed Mar. 2024. https://scholar.google.com/citations?view_op=view_citation&hl=en&user=6cIIBgIAAAAJ&citation_for_view=6cIIBgIAAAAJ:2osOgNQ5qMEC.

Verduin, Leonard. *Reformers and their Stepchildren.* Grand Rapids, MI: Eerdmans Publishing Co., 1964.

Vine, W. E. *An Expository Dictionary of New Testament Words with their Precise Meanings for English Readers.* Old Tappan, NJ: Revel Company, 1966.

Viola, Frank and George Barna. *Pagan Christianity?: Exploring the Roots of Our Church Practices.* Carol Stream, IL: Tyndale House Publishers, 2008.

Warren, Rick. *The Purpose-Driven Church: Growth without Compromising your Message and Mission.* Grand Rapids, MI: Zondervan, 1995.

Wilkerson, David and John and Elizabeth Sherrill. *The Cross and the Switchblade.* Bernard Geis Associates, 1963.

Willard, Dallas. *The Spirit of the Disciplines: Understanding How God Changes Lives.* San Francisco, CA: Harper and Row, 1988.

Willis, Avery T. and Henry T. Blackaby. *On Mission with God: Living God's Purpose for His Glory.* Nashville, TN: Broadman & Holman Publishers, 2002.

Wood, Michael Shane and Dail Fields. "Exploring the Impact of Shared Leadership on Management Team Member Job Outcomes." *Baltic Journal of Management,* vol. 2, iss.3 (2007) Accessed Mar. 2024. https://www.proquest.com/docview/208674357/75EC6B4410B64EB-9PQ/1?sourcetype=Scholarly%20Journals

www.ingramcontent.com/pod-product-compliance
Lightning Source LLC
Chambersburg PA
CBHW050551160426
43199CB00015B/2616